THE NEW GUARD
LITERARY REVIEW

P.O. BOX 10612
PORTLAND, ME 04104
www.newguardreview.com

Writers for writers' sake.

PUBLISHER, EDITOR-IN-CHIEF
& FOUNDER
Shanna Miller McNair

JUDGES
Donald Hall
Debra Spark
CONSULTING EDITOR
Jesse Miller
EDITORS IN FICTION
Erin Enberg
Melissa Falcon Field
Jesse Miller
Shanna Miller McNair
Brandi Neal

EDITORS IN POETRY
Jenny Doughty
Shanna Miller McNair
COPYEDITORS
Jesse Miller
Shanna Miller McNair
David Scribner
Sherry Whittemore
TYPESETTING
Jenn Harrington
COVER DESIGN
Jeremiah Hackett

VIDEOGRAPHY
Patrick Rioux
ANIMATION
Diana Choksey
MERCHANDISE ART
Sergei Chaparin
WEB DESIGN
David Lydon
WEB ART
James Provenzano
Liza Provenzano

Copyright © 2010 by *The New Guard*

Cover painting: *The Model School*, 2008, oil on canvas © E. Kendra Denny

All written material in this issue is in its first publication. *The New Guard* retains standard first publication rights; all rights revert to the writer upon publication. This publication may not be reproduced, stored in a retrieval system, or transmitted in any form or by any other means, electronic, mechanical or otherwise, without written permission of the publisher.

For book orders please visit www.newguardreview.com

Printed by Kase Printing, Inc. Hudson, NH

The New Guard would like to extend warmest thanks to Portland Arts & Cultural Alliance (PACA) of Portland, Maine, for their support and fiscal sponsorship as we await 501(c)(3) status.

ISBN: 978-0-615-42808-6

First Edition, Volume 1

In loving memory of Alice Bloom

Table of Contents

Editor's Note

Writers to Writers: Fan Letters to the Dead

Sven Birkerts to	Julio Cortázar	1
Adam Braver to	Wallace Stevens	3
Boman Desai to	Agatha Christie	4
Annie Finch to	Enheduanna of Sumer	6
John Goldbach to	Marcel Proust	7
Tom Grimes to	Frank Conroy	9
Richard Hoffman to	e. e. cummings	10
Maxine Kumin to	W. H. Auden	12
Thomas Lynch to	William Carlos Williams	14
Josip Novakovich to	Heinrich von Kleist	16
Lewis Robinson to	Emily Dickinson	17
Afaa Michael Weaver to	Frederick Douglass	18
Scott Wolven to	Jim Thompson	19

❊

Fish Story	Payne Ratner	21
Morning	David Crews	32
Road Trip, 1983	Michael Schmeltzer	33
Herman and Laurie in Retrospect	Elisa Pulido	35
China	Harry Newman	38
The Lovers Set Down Their Spoons	Heather A. Slomski	40
The Eff Off Villain Elles	Jen Karetnick	52
Tattoo	Michael Pearce	56
Asante	Matt Miller	58
Coldbrook	J. Preston Witt	61
Odds	Michael Bazzett	71
The Numbers	Hal LaCroix	72
Collateral	Kevin Carollo	74
The Nice Guy	Jaed Coffin	76
Cheers	Lynn McGee	85
The Tasmanian Wolf, and You	Lynn McGee	87
Stray	Allison Alsup	89
Story of Simultaneity	Rachael Lyon	96

Table of Contents

The Habits of Phonies and Living Things [Exhibits]	Alyssa Barrett	98
nichos	Jodie Marion	110
His Eye	Penelope Scambly Schott	111
the music lesson—december 1943	Marcia Popp	112
Saturday's Child Remembered	Eileen Annie	113
The Muse	Judith Podell	115
Women and Men	Christina M. Rau	128
Sightings	George Drew	129
Amateur Night at the Conscience Club	Bradford Winters	131
The Air Around Her Objects	Jefferson Navicky	133
A Red Chair	William Derge	140
Creation: The Madlib Version	James K. Zimmerman	143
Disambiguation	Cary Waterman	145
Early Girl	Elinor Benedict	147
The Cold Front	Erica Plouffe Lazure	148
Cancer	Thoreau Raymond	157
Still Falling	Matt Miller	158
Windflower	Bill Roorbach	160
Outdoor Sermon on the Concrete Foundation of What Was the First Baptist Church of Gulfport, Mississippi	Jacob Newberry	172
mowing	Ken Taylor	175

✷

Winners, Finalists and Contributors	178
Acknowledgements	189

CONTEST ANNOUNCEMENTS

WINNER OF THE MACHIGONNE FICTION PRIZE

(Judge: Debra Spark)
Payne Ratner for FISH STORY

WINNER OF THE KNIGHTVILLE POETRY PRIZE

(Judge: Donald Hall)
William Derge for A RED CHAIR

FINALISTS IN FICTION

Allison Alsup	STRAY
Alyssa Barrett	THE HABITS OF PHONIES AND LIVING THINGS [Exhibits]
Erica Plouffe Lazure	THE COLD FRONT
Jefferson Navicky	THE AIR AROUND HER OBJECTS
Judith Podell	THE MUSE
Heather A. Slomski	THE LOVERS SET DOWN THEIR SPOONS
J. Preston Witt	COLDBROOK

FINALISTS IN POETRY

Eileen Annie	SATURDAY'S CHILD REMEMBERED
Michael Bazzett	ODDS
Kevin Carollo	COLLATERAL
David Crews	MORNING
Jen Karetnick	THE EFF OFF VILLAIN ELLES
Lynn McGee	THE TASMANIAN WOLF, AND YOU
Matt Miller	ASANTE
Harry Newman	CHINA
Michael Pearce	TATTOO
Elisa Pulido	HERMAN AND LAURIE IN RETROSPECT
Michael Schmeltzer	ROAD TRIP, 1983
Ken Taylor	mowing
Cary Waterman	DISAMBIGUATION

CONTEST ANNOUNCEMENTS

SEMI-FINALISTS IN POETRY

George Drew	SIGHTINGS
Hal LaCroix	THE NUMBERS
Rachael Lyon	STORY OF SIMULTANEITY
Jodie Marion	nichos
Lynn McGee	CHEERS
Matt Miller	STILL FALLING
Jacob Newberry	OUTDOOR SERMON ON THE CONCRETE FOUNDATION OF WHAT WAS THE FIRST BAPTIST CHURCH OF GULFPORT, MISSISSIPPI
Marcia Popp	the music lesson—december 1943
Christina M. Rau	WOMEN AND MEN
Thoreau Raymond	CANCER
Penelope Scambly Schott	HIS EYE
Bradford Winters	AMATEUR NIGHT AT THE CONSCIENCE CLUB
James K. Zimmerman	CREATION: THE MADLIB VERSION

Editor's Note

I founded *The New Guard* in hopes of uncovering something bold and unusual—maybe even a new form—by juxtaposing the narrative with the experimental. Give me a story, a rippin' yarn, whatever your genre, and dig into your wildest self to make it all happen. The writers inside this issue did just that, and the work on these pages makes me feel like the world is just a little bit better and bigger, and that making art is just a little bit more possible. To be able to print it all is a joy, of course. Especially since the review was also born of a desire to support fellow writers through print publication: even the larger publishing entities are collapsing, and it gets harder and harder for writers to get their work onto the printed page. That, and I am biased. I love books. A book is a perfect object, I say, and may be the best way of being inside one's own mind, learning, reveling, dreaming, thinking. So, together here in Maine, a group of writers and artists created *The New Guard*, and made the volume you are now holding in your hands.

In Donald Hall's final note on winners and finalists, he said, "if you have the opportunity, please tell everybody that I liked everything, but that I had promised to pick one in particular." He also mentioned running themes in the finalist poems, such as the use of numbering. Still more threads run through the greater book—existentialism and loss, the arc of epiphany and there are wonderful punctuations made by the color red. There is also a veritable zoo in between these covers; this book is a kind of ark. It seems to me the ark is *TNG*'s silent story, since Melissa Falcon Field (Fiction Editor) gave birth to a baby boy during the creation of *TNG* and named him "Noah," my husband Jesse's newly-finished novel is called *Ark*, and my parents, Wes and Diane, have collected miniature two-by-two animals for their so-called "anniversary ark" each year for many of their marriage's 48 years. There are also many birds within these pages, which underscore our review's first flight.

More than anything, this book feels like a living metaphor. Maybe it's yet more than that. As my late mentor Alice Bloom used to say, agog at the natural world, or a person's mind, or some gorgeous work of writing or art, "This is art, with a capital 'A.'" I remember her saying that books are Art with a capital A. I think Alice would be proud of this book. I know that I am.

—Shanna Miller McNair
Knightville, Maine 2010

Writers to Writers: Fan Letters to the Dead

Dearest Julio,

 The temerity, the *hubris*, of using personal address with a man I've never met! I could try to argue that after death the metaphysics of address change, though I'm not sure why that would be. More to the point: enough years have passed since I read you and incorporated your sensibility. Time itself has made you familiar. One cannot live with an influence for thirty years and expect that the formalities of etiquette apply. I'm guessing that you would agree with me. After all, what first drew me to your sensibility was its antic, anarchic quality. You were all about confounding plans, administering the Zen slap, finessing the metaphysical pratfall, bending over to position the banana peel right where the self-important one was about to step. So.
 I'm thinking about you often these days, and for several reasons. The deepest, I suppose, is that I find myself doing a lot of reckoning—in my writing, in my life—trying to determine what has lasted and what hasn't, and in each case, why. How do we measure an influence? Hard to say. At one point, decades ago, you were everywhere in my prose. I could go to early pages now and mark the phrases out one after the next. That changed. I flatter myself to think that I grew a voice of my own. Does that mean I have shed you, lost you? No, more likely I have somehow metabolized your influence.
 Prose style is one thing, but mind and spirit are another. When I was in my twenties you stood for so many things, all of them the components of my day-dreamy romanticism. From your stories, from *Hopscotch*, I took—well, let me dump the bag on the table. I took: the fantasy of Paris, jazz, exile, the idea that there are paths—life paths—that move through books, Surrealism, Malcolm Lowry (you quoted him and a hundred others), bridges, tramps, the stop-time of photography, the metaphysics of coincidence, the power of games, destinies…I am just getting started. I took the idea that writing is not an occupation but a metaphysical vocation. As is reading.
 I was in a bookstore in Cambridge yesterday with my daughter. She is twenty-two and in love with writing and reading. I always want to be giving her books. I saw a paperback copy of *Hopscotch* on a display table. "You have this, right?" I asked. She said she did, but had loaned it to a friend and that she didn't know when she might get it back. I said I

I

would buy her another copy. I wanted her to have it on hand. She shook her head and smiled. "Do you realize that you always give me the books that you wanted?" She was exactly right. I remain earnest about the connections that happen when we read, that *can* happen—not just in the time of reading, but in the time that unfolds from reading. Oh dear, this was meant to be a fan letter, but it has become a meandering instead, like one of those afternoons you describe so often, that starts with the plan to buy a string of sausages at the corner butcher's, say, and ends with the character somewhere way across town listening to a gypsy accordionist, dinner forgotten. Happy.

    Thank you.
    Sven

Writers to Writers: Fan Letters to the Dead

Dear Mr. Stevens,

    I am not typically prone to writing this kind of letter, but I was afraid that if another day passed, I might lose the initiative and forget to thank you for your wonderful work. You see, Mr. Stevens, sometimes one finds oneself in unexpected places in life—suddenly and without anticipation. (But I don't have to tell you that. Isn't that the heart of your line of work?) What I'm getting at is that just when one believes things are hopeless, almost out of the blue can come something to make you believe that everything could be normal again—well, if not normal then at least passable. And, if I may, that is what you've done for me.

    Without boring you with specifics (and keeping brevity in mind), I'll remind you that our paths crossed when an issue concerning my elimination period had been suggested by your company. The idea of the waiting period that your claims adjuster had determined seemed rash. In fact, I found all of his so-called readings on my policy erring toward the inhumane (and I'm not even including the intolerable and immeasurable back-and-forths regarding issues of Exposures, Hazards, Perils and Loss Ratios, Total Loss, Stop Loss, Waivers and Valuation Reserves). I had then demanded that someone with more measure review my case. That's how my problems ended up on your desk.

    In a simple memo, Mr. Stevens, you adjudicated my rightful indemnity. You wrote lovingly of the implied protections of an Umbrella Policy. You carefully considered how the Named Perils and the Hazardous Activities are, by their own rights, Exclusions, and that one should not think of the Risk Class as a Surrender, but perhaps as a direct question of what is and what is not an Act of God. I believe you concluded by saying something to the effect of "After the final no there comes a yes and on that yes the future of the world hangs." And how true that is, Mr. Stevens. Because whether you're aware of it or not, through your careful deliberations, you have given me a "future."

    I know you're a busy man, Mr. Stevens. But I just want to thank you. And while I know so much of what you do concerns other peoples' complications, I hope you know you have a way of making them all make sense.

    Sincerely yours,
    Adam Braver

WRITERS TO WRITERS: FAN LETTERS TO THE DEAD

My dear Dame Agatha,

I beg your pardon, but I speak with the greatest affection and admiration though you would be first to pooh-pooh what I say. In 1930, stepping into your second marriage, in the wake of ten novels, among them *The Murder of Roger Ackroyd*, arguably the cleverest murder mystery ever written, you still considered yourself primarily a "married woman," books your sideline, and "career" much too grand a word for what you did. When your new mother-in-law suggested you write something *serious*, you said you were not really an author! *Dame* Agatha! Not really an author? *You?!* Just for the record, you've sold more than four billion books. Only the Bible leads you (with the advantage of Divine Intervention) and Shakespeare (with the advantage of 400 years). You are the most translated author ever, and your play, *The Mousetrap*, which opened in 1952, still runs after 23,000+ performances, the runner-up so far behind it might as well be the 100th runner-up. You have written more books, each of which might individually have made your name, than any other author—but these are mere statistics, you were trying only to entertain, this is not "serious" work, not what your shining mother-in-law might have wanted. Sorry, but you're wrong. Hear me out.

Granted, you were a leaden stylist, your plots potboiled, your characters made of sticks. How many murders could there possibly have been in those sleepy hamlets and parishes, so neatly plotted and resolved? But people who raise those issues understand nothing. They criticize the perfectest apple for not being an orange. I won't bother to answer them. I will say instead that you taught me to appreciate Shakespeare better than any pompous professor. I never understood hoary old Othello, killing Desdemona on the evidence of a misappropriated handkerchief, until you indicated in *Peril at End House* that the handkerchief was only the final straw, hardly the entire bale. Age was against Othello, experience was against Othello, and he knew it, just as he knew that neither age nor experience were against Cassio, whose age and experience almost exactly overlapped Desdemona's—and that, more than the handkerchief, was the poison working against Othello.

You also indicated how perfectly Shakespeare suited characters to plots. Hamlet, inhabiting Othello's play, would have procrastinated the murder long enough for truth to emerge, but there would then have been no play. Othello, inhabiting Hamlet's play, would have run Claudius through at his prayers when he had the chance in the third act, pious Hamlet did not, imagining death at prayer would send Claudius to heaven, but a play of three acts was a play cut in half.

You had your finger on Shakespeare's essence, you understood human nature as Shakespeare understood human nature, but Shakespeare used his understanding to expose the soul, and you to expose murderers. The principle was the same, the venue different, and there is a great deal to be learned from your books that writers with silverier tongues avoid at their peril, litterateurs too snobbish to recognize that Jesus dressed in rags and Herod in satins and velvets.

There is so much more I could say—each book offers wisdom for those enterprising enough to look—but let me scoop just the top off the aphorisms we (including your sainted mother-in-law) would do so well to remember: (1) *If the fact will not fit the theory—let the theory go*; (2) *Every murderer is probably somebody's old friend*; and my favorite, especially as I get older; (3) *The young people think the old people are fools—but the old people* know *the young people are fools*. These serve us as well in life as in death by murder.

I could go on, but my point is made, and if it's not been made it will never be made. You stand on the shoulders of Shakespeare as much as he smiles over yours, and I remain floundering in the wake of your red herrings.

Your acolyte,
Boman Desai

Hymn to Enheduanna of Sumer

Mother of poets, Enheduanna, the first published poet,
Life-giving mother of Sappho, of Dickinson, of Tsvetaeva!
Mother of Brooks and Lorde, of H.D. and Millay,
You reach towards all of us from the beginning, from the desert,
Mother of poets, daughter and priestess of Inanna!

Life-giving, word-giving, priestess of "the Radiance,"
You of the "honey-sweet voice" and the "bitter fate,"
Though you were forced "among the mountain thorns,"
Though you died in an "inimical land," "singing the holy song,"
Your words have come down from the darkness of four thousand years!

They shine on us again, with the flaming of your Goddess,
You whose tears were sweet drinks for Inanna to drink,
You who praised Her and still wrote down your own name
On the stone tablets that speak of her "joyous allure,"
Her "fierce countenance," her "contentiousness and disobedience."

    —Annie Finch

Writers to Writers: Fan Letters to the Dead

Mon cher M. Valentin Louis Georges Eugène Marcel Proust,

Yr name, btw, is totally awesome! Yr long novel, too, kicks major ass! I've had some relationships go bad, like everybody, and you write so well about such things, etc. I read *À la recherche du temps perdu* in English but I read some French b/c I grew up in Canada and took some French classes but didn't really pay much attention and the classes weren't very good but one day I'll read the whole thing in French, for sure, since you know so much about desire and time and write so beautifully (e.g., in *La Prisonnière*, you write, "Love is space and time made perceptible to the heart"), etc. I know a lot of people have written you letters. I know, e.g., that André Gide wrote to you saying, *Mon cher Proust, depuis quelques jours je ne quitte plus votre livre; je m'en sursature avec délices, je m'y vautre. Hélas! pourquoi faut-il qu'il me soit si douloureux de tant l'aimer?* And didn't he originally refuse to publish *Du côté de chez Swann*? I read once that you met James Joyce and you asked him if he liked truffles and he said *yes I do* but I also read once that you met James Joyce and the only word you guys exchanged was *non*, the answer you both gave when asked if you'd read each others work. But I also read once that James Joyce was at a party thrown for Diaghilev and Stravinsky, celebrating a ballet they wrote or something, in Paris and Joyce was w/o a dinner jacket b/c he couldn't afford one and then you arrived, wearing expensive furs, and I read that you hadn't been on the scene for a while b/c you were working hard on yr novel in yr cork-lined bedroom and yr health was failing, and I remember reading that Joyce was nervous to meet you so he over-compensated for his social anxiety by drinking too much, which he was often wont to do, which many are often wont to do, and that later in the night you were getting into a cab, w/ some friends, and Joyce hopped in, jacketless, and he was nervous and drunk so he lit a cigarette and rolled down the window— both smoke and draughts being bad for yr horribly debilitating asthma (doesn't yr narrator suspect Albertine of leaving a window open on purpose before leaving him for good?)—and when the cab arrived at yr flat you asked the cab to continue on w/ Joyce, thereby excluding him from the small impromptu get-together you were having at yr apt. Is this version of the story true? I know you weren't well at the time and Joyce was probably hammered but this story always saddens me a little but I get it and don't hold it against you. But supposedly Joyce really wanted to talk to you. I don't know. When you died in Nov. of '22, however, he attended yr funeral…*Voilà qui est dit*, reading and rereading the volumes of yr long novel's such a great experience (really, truly, an experience!) and you're definitely one of my all-time faves! *En vérité, je vous remercie beaucoup! Vous êtes un grand maître…Croyez, cher Monsieur, à mes sentiments affectueux et dévoués…*

—J.G.

Dear Frank,

　　I've written a memoir about friendship. I never expected to. Most people love the book, and I receive a lot of mail regarding it. The memoir is also about our lives as writers. (One reviewer, however, said that writers who read it might be tempted to commit suicide, another said that anyone who plans to become a writer has to read it. The latter won a Pulitzer for journalism. I'll trust his opinion.)
　　It's odd how similar our lives turned out to be. You wrote a memoir that changed your life; now I've written one that's changed mine. But a strange thing has happened, and maybe you experienced this too, after you completed *Stop-Time*. My book has silenced the demons that have haunted me for twenty years, and has closed off my past so completely that I no longer seem to have one. But I'm not writing now because I can't see my future. I'm in limbo, which is perhaps how you felt. The paradox for me is that while my past is gone, you're more present in my life than you've been in years.
　　I don't know how long the two stacks of your books—multiple copies in some cases, including a signed first edition of *Stop-Time* that an anonymous reader sent me as a gift after reading your memoir—will sit on the corner of my desk, their titles facing me, just as a photograph of you stares at me above my laptop screen as I type. They've been there for two years now. I want to move on, but I can't let you go, even though you might prefer to have your books back on the shelf.
　　So, we're stuck with one another. I wrote about our sixteen-year long friendship. Now it's gone on for more than twenty. But I don't see it ending until I die and, for me, time finally stops.

　　Tom

Writers to Writers: Fan Letters to the Dead

Dear Estlin,

Writing to say thanks for being such a reliable companion for so long. When I was a kid, just a high school kid, I came across one of your poems and it winked and poked me and tickled me and made me feel in the know about lovemaking when I didn't know the first thing about it. Oh, I had seen some pretty explicit pornography, but I didn't have the tiniest idea what screwing not just somebody but a lover might feel like. What could this flushed adrenalized passion have to do with the adoration and affection I felt for that girl Joanie in my American Literature class? I thought *i like my body when it is with your body* just about said it. It saved me, there in my text in English, from the broken bloody body hanging in the front of the room above the nun's starched head. I gave the poem to Joanie and, oh boy, we gave each other to each other as much as a couple of Catholic schoolkids could without going to hell. So I learned, I think, how a poem can come alive in a life. Thanks for that. May I never forget it.

I'm writing from Cambridge, near your old neighborhood. My kids went to the Agassiz school where you learned to read and write. The joke goes that they still don't know how to capitalize.

And I'm writing while staring at your self-portrait, the one where you're smoking your pipe and holding a notebook and pencil. Were you writing or drawing? I like your paintings. I used to head up to 47th Street in New York where they had your paintings, on that street of diamonds, above the Gotham Book Mart. "Wise Men Fish Here" it said on their sign. I caught several more of your books there, carried them with me to demonstrations against the Vietnam War. I started to see, I think, that the more ways one can express love in words, and in paint, the more ways one can love, something like the way that knowing the names of the trees changes a walk in the woods. And I saw that one form of love is defiance of the shamed, unloving world, of the ignorant acquiescence to brutality. So I saw another thing that poetry might do, and that all poems are love poems.

I just read *i sing of Olaf glad & big* for maybe the hundredth time and I wish he were here now, when there doesn't seem to be any shit

Americans will not eat. Not only that but they pay for it, willingly, enthusiastically. The newspapers are all one big ad for it.

So, again, thank you. I'm going to sign off. Have to get back to this love poem I'm working on. It's an angry one.

Warmly,
Richard

Dear Wystan (if I may),

Imagine this aging feminist taking a dead white male as a role model! It feels almost traitorous in the 21st century of equality for women, a cause to which I have been devoted from the outset. At Radcliffe in the nineteen forties, I didn't meet a single female graduate assistant, instructor, or professor. The only poetry course I took, labeled a modern survey, stopped with Siegfried Sassoon.

I will be honest. Gender had nothing to do with my passion. I dutifully read and admired Bishop and Moore. But I fell in love with your trochees, your trimeter and tetrameter lines, your agility with metaphor and rhyme so vividly represented in the elegy for Yeats. Of course I memorized it, returning over and over to "In the nightmare of the dark/ All the dogs of Europe bark…," that seamless melding of ideational content and metaphor. That was how I wanted to sound someday.

Your tightly furled outrage voiced in "September 1, 1939," the day on which the Nazis marched into Poland and World War II began, stood as a beacon in its time. You didn't put it through a dozen revisions—*The New Republic* published it barely six weeks later.

When we were undergrads we sat around reciting; "I sit in one of the dives/ On Fifty-second Street/ Uncertain and afraid/ As the clever hopes expire/ Of a low dishonest decade…" It remains my favorite poem, right up there with Yeats's "Easter 1916," even though you dismissed it, loathed it, and banished it from your *Collected Poetry*. Most anthologies have restored it, complete with the offending line, "We must love one another or die," which you first emended to "We must love one another and die" before you consigned the entire poem to your personal rubbish heap.

I was lucky enough to attend two of your public readings, one at Boston College, I believe in the late fifties or early sixties. In those days we poet wannabes arrived with the poet's books and as he (it was almost always a he) announced the title of the poem, we raced to find the page so we could follow along. By then your British accent was beginning to elide here and there into American pronunciation. You slouched, deceptively casual, as you entered from stage right. I was enthralled, too, by your insouciance as you crossed to the podium wearing carpet slippers. Looking back over the archives of The Auden Society I see that you read in May of 1939 at Bennington College, then an all-female institution. Hardly a trace of that event remains, alas, so I cannot find when wearing slippers became your way of going. Although you returned to Bennington to teach in 1945, your footwear escaped mention. I wish I had the courage to emulate you in public.

    Farewell, Wystan. I feel blessed to have been allowed this last letter between us. It is a privilege "to serve this unpopular art which…/ cannot be 'done' like Venice/ or abridged like Tolstoy, but stubbornly still insists upon/ being read…"

    MK

Writers to Writers: Fan Letters to the Dead

Doctor Williams,

    This is just to say I never really got it—that part about so much depending upon a red wheelbarrow, etcetera: the glaze of rain water, the white chickens—a fetching mystery, but a mystery nonetheless. I was young when I first encountered it. I counted everything, examined the pattern of stressed and unstressed syllables, after a while just let it be: a little chaser for that one about the plums and the icebox and pleading forgiveness for having eaten them which, needless to say, I took to heart quite readily. I'd give out with bits and pieces of your poems, now and then, to win the attentions of comely girls, some of whom actually seemed to understand.

    But things happen. The ante gets irretrievably upped by life as we come to know it. Things happen, as you know yourself, without rhyme or reason.

    One winter we had two boys go through the ice on the river that runs through town, two brothers, not twins but near enough. The pair of them fit side by side, the older boy's arm around the younger one's shoulder, decked out in their *OshKosh B'Gosh* bib overall jeans their mother had mail-ordered for them for Christmas. Six and four, or seven and five? Either way, they both fit inside the one coffin I could not charge their father for. I remember standing beside that box in the little parlor, those poor hollow parents, holding each other upright, her god-awful sobs, low and animal, and me there with them for what we call, in my line of work, the first viewing. I was not yet thirty and thought I'd seen everything—as if seeing one was seeing all. And I turned to look out the window on the east side of the parlor into the grey mid-December light, the bald trees up and down East Street, on Liberty the daily traffic undisturbed, the Presbyterian bells on the corner ringing the quarter hour, the shops and cafés and bars on the main drag doing business, and I was searching, Doctor, I remember these near forty years since, looking out over my corner lots, searching for something, anything to let my gaze seize upon upon which everything could be said to depend because looking back into the space I was occupying, that moment, with those damaged parents and those drowned little boys, so sweet, so cold, was, as you know yourself, Doctor, impossible.

    So this is just to say I know you stood with ruined parents, too. And there were things that took your breath away and turned your gaze out of the office windows on your corner of Ridge Road in Rutherford, out across the lawn and gardens, out into the backyard and the old garage where, thanks be to Whoever's In Charge Here, there were the chickens and the wheelbarrow and the rainwater's glaze in which your rheumy eyes found, if neither rhyme nor reason, still momentary repose.

Repose,
T. Lynch

Writers to Writers: Fan Letters to the Dead

Guten Morgen, Heinrich!

That is, if there are mornings in the afterlife. Now for several years I wanted to write to you to tell you something that has been bothering me. Namely, why the hell does even your death sound like a story? It's so amazingly well-staged in a beautiful setting, at Wannsee, under a willow tree, that it's hard for me to believe that you didn't write the account. I visited the place where now people sail and sun-starved northern German girls sunbathe topless, and I wonder how many of them think of you and your suicide pact with your ill girlfriend. Were you only helping her and making sure she did not feel alone as she exited this life in your violent kind of euthanasia? Or were you sick of life and you wanted to exit it in good company? But let me tell you one thing: all the stories you wrote, each one of them, is better than the script of your suicide. It's too bad that your worst story cost you your life. I think you are the best short story plotter ever, so I am not surprised that even your death was plotted by you. So you drank 30 cups of coffee before dissing yourself? Well, those days, from what I read, the coffee was pretty watery, and if it tasted anything like diner coffee in the States, I think suicide would be better than 30 cups of it. And then you drank 10 bottles of red wine? Now that is a little excessive. That is how much Alexander the Great drank, and that was enough to finish him off. And he drank strong southern wine. I imagine you drank some awful German red wine. I've never had luck with German reds from the north. I imagine drinking weak red wine would be depressing too. Plus, didn't the waiters try to cheat you and mix the wine with water? Anyway, sometimes I feel guilty when I write a poor story. I should feel guilty more often, but to die for conceiving a mediocre short story, my friend? I do think you went freaking too far. God, and just to think of it, after you left, Goethe was alone as the king and he could not write one single good story—lots of fine hot air and poetry, but not a single story that would be even as good as your suicide. I keep re-reading your stories and they keep getting better and better for me. Pardon the old wine cliché. Still, I want to ask you, how much of your suicide is real? And how much of it is fiction? I miss you, mein Freund, but I don't want to see you for at least fifty years.

Cheers,
Josip

Emily! I'm expecting you!
Just last Night
Had a dream
That hinted you were due—

The Frogs are Fast asleep Now—
Frozen, under Leaves—
Birds, all South—
The crabgrass crusted with rime—

But this dream—it was wild!
You, in your white nighty
Reporting warm, thick Clover
And Frogs coming Home, off to Work.

Keep checking your email
And shoot me one back.
Or better, stop by—

Yours,
Lewis

Dear Mr. Douglass,

    To say I am in awe of all that you managed to accomplish would be something of an understatement. My words would be clearer if imagined from my workplace in a factory across from where you lived until you escaped to freedom. For the better part of fifteen years I worked across the harbor in Locust Point at a soap factory. Well, a soap factory for sure, but more properly it is what some of the plantations of your time became, multinational corporations. In any event, there I was on a harbor point due south and less than a mile away from where you lived and worked. In my own struggles as a black man making a literary life in post-slavery America, I have so often thought of you and felt inspired, lifted up, as they say. What courage you had, and how similar some obstacles remain for black people in this country. More importantly, how different this country would have been had you not given of yourself in the way that you did. You struggled against the inhumanity of the system, and you were strong enough to forgive. You had the prescience to create yourself from that mold you saw within yourself, and we are all the better for it. This American culture has one history in one life that has taken it much closer to its own professed ideals, put its feet to the fire, as black folk say. This is a letter of thanks, of deepest gratitude and admiration. The struggle remains but we are all the better for what you accomplished.

    Sincerely,
    Afaa Michael Weaver

Writers to Writers: Fan Letters to the Dead

Hey Jim—

 I should have written you sooner, but you know how it goes, old buddy. I hope you'll accept this package with my apologies. How are things and what are you drinking these days, south of heaven? I just saw the new version of *The Killer Inside Me*. Man, Jim, what a job they did with that. I heard some of the audience didn't like it and walked out. They couldn't take the violence. For Lord's sake, those poor people must never watch the news. Anyway, Casey Affleck is Lou Ford and the kid is brilliant, Jim, just brilliant. It's the genuine article. Equal to *The Grifters*, in my opinion—and we all know that doesn't count for much. It's true to your book, is what I'm saying. That's what matters for me. How did people think a film that was based on one of your books was going to be—pleasant? A quiet walk in park? Not likely. Not by a long shot. The soundtrack has some Texas swing in it, which really adds to the atmosphere. I think you'd like it.

 I got lucky this year and managed to get into an anthology with you. What a thrill. There's my name and yours in the same table of contents. Amazing. But it was really the novels that always got me. I'm sure you've heard those "Dimestore Dostoyevski" and "Firesale Faulkner" comments enough—some of your stuff is absolutely crazy, Jim. I think the French realized it before we caught on here in the US of A. Not many guys have Stephen King writing their forwards—you should keep that in mind, when you feel down.

 You're probably wondering what the rest of the stuff is in this box, all wrapped up. The heavier item, that's a brand new desktop typewriter with extra ribbons and four reams of typing paper. The other items, as I'm sure you can guess by their shape, are a couple bottles of booze, along with some fresh ground coffee. I assume you can get hot water where you are.

 Jim, if you're just sitting around, can you try to crank out one more American masterpiece, before we all head home? It's this world, and then the fireworks and I need one more Jim Thompson before I fold my hand. Get some of this bourbon in you and let's have it—because nobody does it like you, Jim. Thanks, I'll check back in a while.

 Take it easy,
 Scott

Winner of the Machigonne Fiction Contest

Payne Ratner

Fish Story

I'M AT MY DESK AT WORK AND A FISH falls in my lap. It's greasy with water and still flexes. Still alive. The gills pump open and shut.

It twists its head and looks at me and says, Did I make it?

It's so utterly shocking that I'm simply not shocked. I look at it. Watch it begin to die.

Maybe my heart is going a bit fast. I can't tell.

There's a damp grey, soggy spot in the ceiling panel overhead. No hole. Just a bit of a sag.

So then I think, okay, someone's being funny. Some ventriloquist chucked a fish from a rubber bag over the wall of my cubicle. I stand up, look, but no one's looking.

Ha ha, I think, ha fricking ha.

But first things first. This fish needs water.

I don't know if it's fresh or salt, but wet I know for sure will help.

The men's room is right across from me. I take the fish in and plop it in the toilet. It's too big, but at least I get its head and gills in the water so it can breathe.

I stop up the sink and turn on the tap.

What I'll do is get it revived a bit then run it down to the fountain by the Italian restaurant until I can get it to a lake or a pet store.

But this isn't really a pet.

It's an ugly, broke-jawed, mean-looking thing that's scared silly, I bet.

The sink is full and I hear this clap, clap. This weak slap of its tail against the sides of the toilet. I lift it by the tail and ease it in the sink water. It's pretty limp but the sink is too small for it to turn its belly up so I think that's a good thing. If its belly can't go up it can't die.

I think, I'm spending more time on this fish than I have on my marriage in five years.

Mitch Wardenstone comes in.

Whatcha got there? he says.

He leans over so I smell his lunch.

It's a fish, he says.

He goes into the stall, sits down. Waits for a second. Then he comes out.

I don't know why I went in there, he said.

Then he goes to the urinal and stands there for five minutes while I watch the fish twitch a little, see its gills work half way.

He's back there and he's not pissing.

Oh, well, he says.

He zips up and comes over.

It's this goddamn medication, he says.

He looks in the sink.

How'm I gonna wash my hands, he says.

You can use the kitchenette, I say, the little sink in there.

Oh, yeah.

He takes hold of the handle.

See you at the meeting, he says.

Oh, shit, I say, when's it start, again?

Like, he says. He looks at his watch. Like now.

Shit, I say, I still need to print that shit.

It's not printed?

I was going to now, but this.

I look at the fish. It looks a little better but the drain doesn't hold and the sink is half empty.

Fish Story

Can you watch this thing, I say.
The fish?
Like, two minutes.
What's it gonna help to watch it?
Just give it a little water when it starts to run out.
Okay, but hurry.
I go out, pull up the document, hit print, go back in.
The water's almost gone. The fish has a panicked look on its face. Mitch is standing in front of the urinal. I turn on the tap.
I gotta talk to this asshole doctor of mine, Mitch says.
He zips up.
Still nothing, he says. But the urge. It's like Hoover Dam, he says.
Tell them I'll be there in a second, I say.
I look down and the fish gives me this pathetic don't-ever-leave-me-look and I know I'm sunk.

What're you doing home my wife says.
Her boyfriend comes in behind her. Carl. All shoulders and neck.
Hi, Carl, I say.
Hi, Tom.
I kinda got a situation at work, I say.
What kinda situation, she says.
I'm gonna take a shower, Carl says.
The mail? She says.
Oh, yeah.
He hands her a stack of bills and glossy ads, drops his coat on the Lazy Boy, and goes off to the bathroom.
The guy takes more showers than a rain forest, my wife says.
He's self-conscious about his glands, I say.
That's all psychological, she says.
But things ooze out of him, I say, tropical oils.
That's a load of crap, she says, he's a sloppy eater, period.
Why d'you stay with him, I say.
You don't want to know, she says.
I do.
My mom's new boyfriend, Tom the shrink, says if it wasn't for Carl, I'd be too afraid to stay with you. He says Carl's all about 'cause I love you so much.

23

Great way to show it, I say.

I know, I'm sorry, it's just, you know, I don't know, whatever.

Why's he say I put up with it? I say.

He can't figure that out, she says.

She sits on the sofa, pops off her shoe with her toe.

Oh, God, what a day, she says. Lady was allergic to one of the perfumes. I sprayed one puff and she went down like I'd shot her through the head. We had to call EMT.

Is she okay?

Yes, but discolored. She looks like a sunset. What's your situation at work?

The bad news is, my situation at work is that I don't have a job, now.

My wife puts her head on the back of the sofa like she's been hit with a hammer.

You better, my wife says, be mother-fucking kidding.

I guess there was some straw somewhere that broke some camel's back, I say.

What the fuck are we gonna do, she says, what in the fucking hell?

I know, I say, I'm sorry.

You know what the landlord said, she says.

I know, I know.

And Carl. Is gonna be so pissed.

Do we have to tell him tonight?

No, she says, we don't. And not because I'm a nice guy. Because the reason is, I want to rip your head off myself.

She bounces the back of her head against the sofa.

Fuck, fuck, fuck, she says.

Then she looks at me.

And how's he gonna buy his medicine? She says.

It's not medicine, I say, it's steroids. Will someone please stop calling it medicine?

Either way, she says, we are seriously fucked. And don't expect me to steal again.

I never wanted you to steal in the first place, I say.

We put our heads back and look at the ceiling. It's hard to believe that she and I ever made love. And she once put her head on my chest and listened to my heart beat.

We are so, so major-league fucked, she says.

But the good news is, I say, is, we got a fish.

Then Carl screams.

Fish Story

It's horrible to hear. Part high-pitched girl in a horror movie, part stuck pig, part man with shrunk testicles.

He stands beside the bathtub with a handful of towel clutched over him. His mouth looks like a raisin.

What the hell's that?

I brought it home from work, I say.

We watch it swish its tail. It spreads some kind of milky cloud around the tub.

What's it doing, spawning? My wife says.

I don't know.

It looks good, though, I think. Happy and healthy. Glossy. Its gills pinked up. It looks like it's grown an inch or two.

Look at this, Carl says.

He sets his foot on the side of the tub. There's a small oval wound.

I think it bit me, he says.

Better wash that out, Dee says.

Can fish have rabies? Carl asks.

He stands at the sink with his leg cocked and lathers up his foot.

What'd they give that for? Like a turkey or something? A ham or something?

It just fell in my lap, I say.

Why didn't you take, like, movie passes, something not so slimy?

It wasn't like a gift they gave me.

What about an iTouch? What's wrong with an iTouch?

Nothing.

Guy at the gym has an iTouch.

Is he gay, I say.

Carl gives me a look.

By ten o'clock Carl's a fish, too.

Dee sits on the toilet and watches them. The two fish circle around and rub each other. The bathroom develops this odor.

It was so weird, Dee says. He was brushing his teeth, then he got this look like something kicked him in the back of the head and then it was like the air going out of a balloon. He went flying all round the room and then plopped in the water. Then there was all this splashing. Next thing you know, there he is.

I look down.

I never seen a fish with blue eyes, I say.

25

Watch when he swims this way, she says.
Oh, my God, I say.
You see the abs?
Jesus, I say.
The bath water explodes and this thing flies out at me. I knock it down on the floor. It lands like a piece of thick, heavy, wet, living rubber that works itself this way and that.
Fucker tried to get me, I say, fucker went for my throat.
He is one pissed fish, Dee says.
She picks him up. He pours out of her hand into the water. Then he turns and glares at me.
If I were you, she said, I would not use this toilet.
I'm going in the kitchen sink, I say.
I would too, she says, and you know how I feel about germs.
You know something, I say, that's the nicest thing you said to me in a long time.

The moon has lit the fuses of all the cats. They're all screaming in pain. One or two pop like firecrackers.
I get off the sofa and go in and look at Dee asleep in bed. As quiet and slow as I can I climb under the sheets, careful not to touch her. I lean on my elbow and watch her breathe.
She opens her eyes and looks at me.
What?
I was thinking, I say, that what if this fish is come to bring us together?
How, she says.
I don't know, I say, stranger things have happened.
Not that strange, she says.
Then she turns her back to me and slowly falls asleep. I stay on the edge all night and think about her body. And fish swimming inside of her.
I ease myself over and whisper in her ear, What about we have a baby?

In the morning I get up, get my old baseball bat from the closet and go in the bathroom. She stands there with her hands across her belly and looks in the tub. I have my bat ready in case I gotta pop it outta the air.

They seem bigger, she says.
They do, I say.
Then the one with Carl's eyes thrashes once and actually puts its head out of the water and stares at me and snaps its gills open and shut. Its face actually gets a little red. Then it slips backward into the water.
The other fish just watches. Cool and silver. With a little silver smile on its face. Like it's got everything under control. Like it's enjoying the show.
What're we gonna feed them?
Fish food, I guess, I say.
You got money, she says.
No. You?
No.
What for food? Like we have bread or something? Something they'd like?
We have that frozen wedding cake, she said.
I thought about that cake, huddled in the corner of the empty freezer, spikes of frost all over it, like the quills of a frightened porcupine. I thought of that day, so full of light and hope.
I don't know, I say, maybe something else.
It'd probably poison them, she said.
I guess, I said.
A jar of salsa.
What do fish eat, anyway?
Fuck, she says, maybe I have to steal.
You are not gonna steal.
I take her by the elbow, I turn her around to look me in the eye.
Do not steal. You want to go to jail? Go to a meeting, I say, but you are not gonna steal. Okay? Promise me.
We gonna let Carl starve?
Just promise me, okay?
I hold her arms. I look at her.
Okay, she says, Jesus, I promise. But what about Hilda?
Hilda, I say, who's Hilda?
That's what I named your fish.
How d'you know it's a girl?
You just do, she says.
Hilda turns, looks up at me. If fish could have long eyelashes, she would. And for a fish, full lips.
I see what you mean, I say.
Dee looks down into the water. She bites white marks in her bottom lip.

Are you jealous? I say.

I'm starving, she says.

After she goes to work I lie on the sofa and watch the spot where the TV used to be. We pawned it last month for food, which was a mistake. Pastor Wallchist said, Man shall not live by bread alone.

At noon the landlord comes by. He knocks hard.

In case anyone's in there, he yells, which I know there is, I'm coming by with the police on Thursday. I got all the legal papers here. I'm sliding 'em under here. For your reading pleasure.

I hear the hiss and crinkle of a fat envelope forced under the door.

I get up, go in the bathroom. The fish are barely moving, like they've been listening.

I turn on the water to get it fresh.

Carl seems less angry. More thoughtful. Hilda has a serious expression on her face. They both bob up to the surface and look at me.

It's okay, I say, there's nothing to worry about.

But you can see they're both worried.

Dee looks half-deflated when she gets home.

You and your fucking promise, she says. We coulda had some buffalo wings and peanuts and some food for the fish but whenever I tried to pick up a little something for us it was like a dog bit me. It wasn't a promise it was a fucking curse.

She peels her sleeve back, there's red marks all over her hand.

I'm sorry, I say, but next time they said was jail.

Three hots and a cot, she says, doesn't seem too bad at the present moment. How're the fish?

I don't know, I fell asleep.

We go in, look at them.

They look depressed, she says.

The landlord came by, I say.

And?

Day after tomorrow.

Dee looks back at the fishes.

Fish Story

You think he'll ever turn back, she says.
That depends, I say, if you love him. Do you love him?
Dee looks back at Carl. He eyes her. He curls his body left, then right, like he was flexing up his biceps. Hilda watches him. She rolls her eyes and turns away.
Dee bursts into tears.
I'm sorry, baby, she says, I'm so sorry.
Are you talking to him or me, I say.
Leave me alone, she says, all of you.

That night for dinner we sit at the table and flip through *Gourmet Magazine*.
Oh, God, Dee says each time we turn a page.
Oh, my god, she says, oh, yeah.
I lay my hand across a sweaty lamb chop.
You're getting me all stirred up, I say.
Get your hand off that chop, she says.
Remember what Pastor Wallchist said, Man shall not live by bread alone.
Just then there's a ruckus in the bathroom. We run in. The water swirls and bucks. Inside the tub the fish have gone from silver scales to a kind of brown. There's a film of water on the floor. Carl launches himself out of the tub, lands on the floor and starts to wriggle towards the door. Then Hilda leaps out and lands in front of him. She squiggles around and slaps him twice across the face. Then she flops around and stares him in the eye. For awhile their mouths flap open and shut, like they're having an argument in a language we can't hear. Then Carl gets this look in his eyes and limps up and falls over on his side. His gills work pretty hard. Dee picks up Carl and I pick up Hilda and we slip them back in the water.

That night I ease into bed while Dee's asleep and lick my fingertip and touch her nipple and watch her face. I think, somehow, I touched the on switch for a dream. I remove my hand and put it in my pocket.
In the morning she says, I can't get up.
Why?
I had a dream.
What kind of dream.

A dream dream, stupid. What other kind is there.
The dream paralyzed you?
How about I haven't eaten in four days? That have anything to do with it?
Boy, you are one serious grouch.
Why can't you have a mother and a father we can mooch off of for awhile? Jesus. What good are you?
Can you tell me what your dream was?
That everything's gonna work out.
And that's why you're upset?
Do you ever listen to anything I say, she said.
I go in the bathroom, check on the fish. They're, like, weaving together. Like, making a braid of water if you could braid water.
Hi guys, I say, how's it going?
But they ignore me.
I go back in.
How are they?
They're acting very strange.
Will you do me a favor, Dee says, will you go look under the green picnic bench in the park and bring back what you find?
Are you serious?
Yes.
And see if you can borrow a phone and tell them I'm not coming in to work.
Today?
Today and maybe tomorrow and maybe not.
Not, what?
She stops talking and nothing I can say will get her started.

It takes me a long time to find the right green bench. They're all green. I hope I found what she wanted. It's a grease-spotted paper bag with a Morton's salt and pepper shaker inside and a lemon.
I get back and she's sitting on the kitchen counter. She looks up.
Her cheeks are red as roosters.
I had a long talk with Carl, she says.
And?
And I think, all his life he's wanted to do something good and strong and courageous but he never knew how. He thought being strong was all about having muscles.

Fish Story

She rubs her eye with the heel of her hand.
Anyway, she says, I think he's ready.
You think?
I don't exactly understand fish, asshole.
Boy, I said.
Think you better talk to Hilda?
Yes.

I go in. She has a hard time staying straight in the water. Carl is facing the corner of the tub.

I lift Hilda out and hold her against my chest. The cold wet slime goes straight to skin and my heart bumps up a beat.

I don't know who you are, I said, or why. But for some reason you've given me something I can't understand.

And then I start to cry. I have no idea why. The tears pop on the water. It's so unusual for me to cry. And to cry so much the tears actually leave my face and hit other parts of the world. Very unusual.

I carry Hilda into the kitchen. Dee hands me a knife.

I'll get Carl, she says.

I lay Hilda on the cutting board. She looks me straight in my eye and I can tell everything is happening as it should.

Dee comes in and lays Carl on the counter. She takes her mother's old hatchet.

She lifts the hatchet, I position the knife.

I feel, I say, like I'm cutting off my thumb.

We eat without a word. We eat 'til we're full. The electricity's shut off half way through dinner but we got the light of a stubby storm candle and the bright sparks of a lemon. When we're done Dee goes into the kitchen and comes out with our old wedding cake. It's still cold, and it's lost a lot of sweet but, still, it's edible.

David Crews

Morning

When I first step out of a hot shower and the heat
      seems to empty from my body, tense

in the half-dark coldness, like that. The bag and things
      you packed. Some of your drawers. Nothing

in the dishwasher or sink, and I need
      more dog food for Murphy. I finished

the fancy coffee because there's no more
      of the regular stuff. Stare at the faded

curtains—somehow the bright white—yellowed,
      dirty. The moldings in the kitchen clot with nicks

and chips. Like that. Like the sunlight rising,
      the open sky, the day slowly emptying,

or taking apart the buttons to empty you out
      of the clothes that once hid your skin, when

I used to touch your face as I emptied
      all of me into you, and then your grip

on my shoulders that filled me with something
      I didn't know I wanted or could need.

Michael Schmeltzer

Road Trip, 1983

My father fills the water bottle
before the bugle call of dawn.

He is meticulous, each suitcase
labeled with our names and address.

Every summer our vacation
begins with a road trip

like a four hour yawn
and my father flushed by noon

with vodka he disguises
as Evian. He spoils us

with gas station snacks:
Moon Pies, Twinkies, the whole family

jawing on jerky. On some
dusty road 90 miles from home

he asks if I want to take the wheel.
I am five and terrified

of tumbleweeds, road kill, the stillness
of an unanswered question.

My mother sleeps
in the backseat, my baby brother

just a bump in her belly.
He is at home wherever she travels,

Michael Schmeltzer

and I am in the old station wagon,
unsure whether to answer

yes or no, what direction
my father is headed, how fast

our house disappears behind us.

Elisa Pulido

Herman and Laurie in Retrospect

1. 1995

Laurie is seventy, has broken her hip.
In the hospital she dreams she is lying on the floor of San Bernardino's train station.

Her father steps off a train in his square-toed boots.
Mosquitoes circle his head, the way they did summers on the Daloney place.

He gathers Laurie into his arms as easily as he did newborn calves on
Wyoming's frozen range, and offers to take her away.

2. 1980

Laurie folds laundry on her kitchen table.
Herman, her father, is ninety-three, is visiting, sitting at the table.

He tells Laurie he and his brothers had to share a single pair of dress shoes.
Sometimes they'd go to church dances.

One brother would wear the shoes into the church, while the other two sat in their socks on a fence, and waited a turn.

Now his wife is gone, Herman tells his own stories.

3. 1970

It's December.
Herman and his wife have taken the train to San Bernardino from Cokeville.

Elisa Pulido

Herman is eighty-three.
He sits in the sunshine on a plastic lawn chair in front of Laurie's pink stucco
 home, and
imagines what he might be missing.

Ice glazing the steps of his front porch.
A row of four-foot icicles.

Through an open window, Herman can hear Minerva telling how one winter, he swam a herd of cattle across the Snake River on horseback.

She says his clothes completely iced over by the time he trailed that herd into Pocatello.

She says he went into a local saloon and stood by a pot-bellied stove, while melt-off from his jacket and trousers, boots and gloves, puddled on the plank floor.

4. *1942*

Skirts, blouses, bobby socks, and a radio—everything a college co-ed will need has been packed into a pale green Mercury.

It is the end of August, 1942.
Laurie and her friends are off to college.

As they drive away from the ranch house, Laurie slides down in her seat so she can't see her father growing smaller.

Herman watches the car cross the tracks, pass the drugstore, the post office, and the Bear River Mercantile.

He watches until the car disappears somewhere past Cozzen's Grocery.

He wonders which day the first snow will fall, thinks about heifers birthing next year's calves in the ice of early spring.

Herman and Laurie in Retrospect

Herman turns, says to Minerva:
Seems like we never had a daughter.

5. 1934

It's early September.
There has already been a frost.

Herman and Laurie drive across sage-covered coke fields to Yamamura's in Kemmerer, where Laurie tries on school shoes.

She'll be in the fourth grade.
Herman buys her a pair of brown leather oxfords—the most expensive pair in the store.

They pinch her toes, dig under her ankles.
She can't bring herself to tell him.

6. 1927

Mosquitoes hide from sun, hunt for mates, arabesque above half-filled irrigation ditches running alongside a gravel lane.

Horses and an empty hayrack jounce toward a freshly-mown field.
It is noon and the rack is hungry.

When it reaches the field, Herman will pitch damp hay onto the rack's empty plate.
Laurie is two, is sitting bare-legged on the bumping rack.
She tries to stand.
Herman steadies her with his ranch-rough hands.

Put a foot here, he says, and one there.
Hold your arms like this.

Harry Newman

CHINA

seek wisdom the Sufi saying goes *even as far as China*
and I think of that because you're on your way again
though they meant a China of the mind the farthest reaches

beyond maps unknowable where silence is the only language
or more the silence within silence so far from words sound
any sense of its opposite the great ocean of thought and breath

we carry within that carries us not the actual China
where you're heading though that too exists beyond itself
seen only as reflections glimpses when the smog clears

I've been thinking lately about oceans their surfaces
changing so quickly never staying still how they remain
essentially unmappable except at coastlines the boundaries

defining what they are not yet even these keep shifting
eroding and building up how little they resemble lines
on the map when we see them only approximation

our feeble dreams of stasis but I'm thinking too
of the oceans around us daily the endless lap
of language of being in new countries like being

under the sea swells of sounds washing over and
around you only with time resolving into currents
waves wavelets crests words phrases sentences

China

we hold onto to keep from drowning piecing together
a lexicon of our own senses meanings repetitions
we hope will carry us these are maps of a kind

personal longitudes internal navigations changing
constantly all we have as we drift from border to border
dreaming of nearer Chinas always beyond our reach

Heather A. Slomski

The Lovers Set Down Their Spoons

WE ARE SITTING AT A TABLE in a restaurant. The four of us. You. Me. The woman with whom you had an affair. Her boyfriend. I sit across from her, you across from her boyfriend. There is wine, red and white. There are four water glasses, four linen napkins, four spoons, eight forks, four knives. There are tables on all sides of us.

Behind the bar a large mirror reflects the brilliance of a chandelier.

The woman with whom you had an affair: (looking at you) How did you find this place?

You: I read a review last week in the paper. The owners live upstairs—they keep a six-hundred-square-foot

The Lovers Set Down Their Spoons

herb garden in planters.

The woman with whom you had an affair: *Six hundred* square feet?

You: Incredible, right?

The woman with whom you had an affair: I'll say.

Her boyfriend: (butters his bread).

The waiter had brought olive oil for our bread, but he, her boyfriend, asked for butter. I liked that about him.

I wonder what he is thinking—the boyfriend—staring now at the couple one table over. She, in a below-the-knee red dress; he, in corduroys and a striped dress shirt. I imagine the boyfriend is wondering if they are lovers. Perhaps if they are both lovers first to someone else, and lovers only second to each other.

She isn't beautiful—the woman with whom you had an affair. Coarse, and a bit squat, she's not at all the woman I'd imagined.

The woman with whom you had an affair: (looking at her menu) Everything looks so good. Good restaurants always make me wish I cooked more. But by the time I even think of dinner it's too late to make anything, so Simon and I usually order in Greek or Thai. (She watches you for your reaction.)

Simon: You hate Thai. You're allergic to peanuts and coconut milk.

The woman with whom you had an affair: (pretends not to hear Simon; she sips her wine and is noticeably relieved when the waiter arrives).

Waiter: (white shirt, black apron, tall and long-limbed) Something more to drink? Perhaps an appetizer?

You: (taking charge) Yes, we'll have the fried sage leaves, and…ahh…(poring over the menu) an order of the squash flan.

Waiter: Very good. (He walks away from the table in long, thin steps.)

The woman with whom you had an affair: Great choices. Simon and I love flan. Don't we, Simon?

Simon: (sips his wine).

You: I order flan whenever it's on the menu.

I notice a slight trembling of the chandelier, as if someone is walking upstairs in the spice cabinet where the owners live, bending between the rows of herbs—plucking.

The waiter arrives with the appetizers and sets them in the middle of the table. You, the orchestrator of this event, lift and reach a sage leaf onto each of our plates with your fork and knife. With your spoon, you slop piles of squash flan next to our sage. The three of us pick up our silverware, but you are unsure of what to do with yours. They've been designated serving utensils. Can you eat from them?

I poke the sage leaf with my fork and bite a third of the leaf. It looks and tastes like a fried anchovy. I grab my water and try to swallow the fish like a vitamin, but I (*cough cough*) choke a little, and spit the fish into my water glass.

You (ignoring me): Oh, this is great. Have you tried the sage (you are looking at her—at the woman with whom you had an affair), have you tried the fried sage leaf?

Through the windows the sun is setting. It is nearing eight o'clock and the last rays are reaching through the glass. They are sliding down the panes like a coat of sheer gold paint, and the restaurant seems to float in this buoyancy of light. I hate New York. I am beginning to feel a sick longing for my before-life—when I lived in Boston and I didn't know you.

Me: Simon. What do you do?

Simon: Taxes (breath). I do taxes.

Me: What do you do for fun?

You, and the woman with whom you had an affair, look at me, simultaneously,

The Lovers Set Down Their Spoons

as if I have just said something wrong, awkward, inappropriate.

Simon: For fun?

Me: Yeah. For fun.

Simon: I play cards, I'm in a bridge club. I golf, go to the movies. Just bought a new bike.

The woman with whom you had an affair: We were in Seattle a couple weeks ago and saw—what is the name of that film (she turns to Simon)—that Spanish one—oh you (she looks from you to me) really have to see it. What was it called, Simon?

Simon: I don't know. I'm glad I forgot. (He looks at me.) If you're into movies where people are so in love with books they masturbate in library bathrooms, then maybe you'd like it. (He sets his fork against his small blue plate.)

You: (looking at her—at the woman with whom you had an affair) Are you talking about the one with *lighting* or *making light* in the title?

Make light, I think. Make light. What words, I wonder, did you use with this woman? Fuck? Have sex? Intercourse? Make love? Make light?

The woman with whom you had an affair: Yes! *Making light of it* or *lighting it*—wait, maybe it was Danish.

Simon: Swedish. (He turns to the table next to us. The woman's fork catches the last of the sun as she lifts it to her lover's lips—if he's even her lover. He almost chokes, and they are laughing.)

The waiter takes our order and when he is finished he closes the sun into his black book. Another waiter hurries around the restaurant holding a cigarette lighter above the tea candle on each table. I watch Simon yawn, and the gold cap on his back tooth twinkles in the candlelight. Something about the gold in his tooth (I turn to look at you) makes me think of the absurdity—the absurdity of us.

You: (to her, of course) Are you reading anything? Anything good?

43

The woman with whom you had an affair: In the last week or so I've accumulated so many new books that Simon and I barely have room to walk.

Simon: (turning briefly from the lovers) I don't have problems walking.

I stand up to find the restroom, but your foot is in the way, so I kick it.

You: (leaning forward) What the—

Me: (I look up at Simon and the woman with whom you had an affair.) Excuse me. (Turning to you) I'm sorry, did I catch your foot?

You: (squinting) That's all right. It was an accident.

Me: Of course it was. (My voice sounds like cranberries.)

Small squares of light drip from the ceiling and illuminate my path to the WC. A few paces ahead, a waiter is slowly approaching. He is balancing two bowls of soup on his right forearm and holding one in his left hand. He looks so young—his red hair sticking up by his ears because someone cut it too short. His belt is the smallest rubber band, holding up his pants like tying a balloon.

Me: (slowly and evenly toned) Careful, I'm right here—right in front of you.

The young waiter: (lifting an eyebrow) I see you.

Me: Do you want me to—

The young waiter: No. I have to do this on my own.

I step aside and he passes by. I watch him walk along his tightrope to deliver the soup. He makes it.

When I am back from the WC, our meals arrive, and the waiter sets them before us, admiring our choices. He leaves, and I look down at my plate. My pasta is green, too pretty to eat. I push my plate forward and reach for the wine bottle. I begin to pour and the waiter rushes over—mortified that my fingers touched the bottle. I wave him away.

The Lovers Set Down Their Spoons

Me: (to you) What?

You: (whispering sternly to me) He would have done that, you know. In places like this you're supposed to let *them* pour your wine.

Me: (to you) Places like *this*? Like *this*? (I'm not sure why the repetition.)

I watch you cut your meat and sprinkle your salt. Sometimes you're a vegetarian and sometimes you're not.

Simon: (taking a bite of his Tre Fungi Penne) This is terrible. I hate mushrooms. (He pushes his plate away.)

The woman with whom you had an affair: I don't know why you ordered it then. (She lifts an asparagus spear to her teeth.)

I had a neighbor, years ago, who cultivated asparagus. Locked out one scorching afternoon, I knocked on his door and asked to use his phone. My boyfriend at the time had the only other key, and when I reached him he told me to stay at the neighbor's or climb through a window. When I repeated this to my neighbor, he said, not many people know this, but asparagus is actually a member of the lily family. Come, I'll show you. We walked through his house and into the garden. That night when my boyfriend brought over the key, I broke up with him. Did you know, I said, that under ideal conditions an asparagus spear can grow ten inches in twenty-four hours? I'd forgotten about my neighbor until tonight.

Simon: I always think, this time, I'll like mushrooms. (He pushes back in his chair and crosses his legs.)

You: (to the table) This lamb is amazing. (*Chew chew chew.*) Mary had a little lamb, little lamb, little lamb? Mary had a little lamb whose tush is on my fork.

The woman with whom you had an affair: (smiling and blushing) That's so mean!

I look to Simon to return my expression, but he's engaged with the lovers.

The lovers: (Her long arms reach across the table for his face, and he drops his chin into her palms).

I've forgotten what it's like to feel a range of emotions in a single day.

Waiter: (bowing) Is something wrong?

Me: Wrong?

Waiter: With your pasta dishes?

I shake my head no, and Simon does the same.

Waiter: (annoyed) Very well. I'll wrap these up.

You and the woman with whom you had an affair finish eating, and the waiter takes our coffee order.

Simon: sugar, no cream.

Me: cream, no sugar.

The woman with whom you had an affair: black.

You: after debating between Earl grey and coffee, you order coffee—black.

The waiter follows his outstretched arms into the kitchen, and a few moments later, appears with a tray of coffees. One by one he lowers a cup and saucer from above each of our heads like birthday cakes we aren't expecting. Then he leaves and returns with the dessert tray.

Waiter: (leaning forward with the tray) This is the raspberry-ginger sorbet. This is the prune tart. This pretty one is the Chinese lantern. This—with the ladyfingers—is the accordion. This is the Brooklyn brownie. And this is a petit madeleine.

The woman with whom you had an affair: (sucking in her stomach and patting it) Just coffee for me.

Simon: (to the waiter) Do you have any lemon tarts?

The Lovers Set Down Their Spoons

Waiter: No, sir. Only what I have here on this tray.

Simon: You're sure there aren't any lemon tarts stuffed in the back of the freezer?

Waiter: No, sir. We only serve homemade desserts that are baked fresh daily.

Simon: What are they having? (He points his thumb at the lovers.)

Waiter: (leaning to the left in order to see past Simon) Looks like they got the last pear flambée. We're discontinuing that dessert after tonight.

I look over to the lovers. Two spoons. Two mouths. Ten fingers—five his, five hers—entwining themselves in each other. A bit over the top, I agree. She reaches for his wrist and turns it toward herself. Clearly they are late for something, because the lovers set down their spoons. They weave through the tables—their raincoats billowing out behind them like the kites you and I flew on that terrible day that began our love. Your kite kept wrapping around mine, and at first I thought it was sweet, but eventually mine nosedived into the sand. I knelt down beside it as the waves crept closer, wanting to take the kite—a small sailboat—out to sea. Your kite was still up in the air and you were balancing yourself beneath it. *Look! Look!* you yelled. *Watch how it twirls!*

I turn around in my chair to face the door, but it's too late. The lovers are gone.

Me: (looking at Simon) Where did they go?

You: Who? Where did who go?

Simon: To a movie.

Me: I doubt it.

You: (to the woman with whom you had an affair) Who are they talking about?

The woman with whom you had an affair: Simon, who are you talking about?

The waiter leans over the table and places the bill in the middle. You and the woman with whom you had an affair begin grabbing at each other's fingers.

You: (swiping the black book from her grip) You bought last time, remember? Those burgers that were bigger than our plates? (With these words you pause, and look at me.)

Me: (whispering) I'm embarrassed.

You: (your hand on my shoulder) I'm sorry. I shouldn't have brought it up. We can still—

Me: I'm embarrassed that you would be interested in someone like her. I'm nothing like her.

You: (looking around for the waiter, because you won—your credit card made it inside the black book and you want him to take it) Of course you're not—there's no one like you. (You raise your hand awkwardly, as if you're hailing a cab for the first time and you're not sure you're doing it right.)

Me: But tell me. I want to know what you saw in her. Oh who am I fooling —what you see in her.

Simon: (pointing at you with his pinky) Hey—I'm embarrassed that she would be interested in someone like him.

You: (pushing back in your chair) Who the hell do you two think you are, anyway?

I laugh out loud.

You: Listen. The affair came about because there were problems, and now there aren't. We're handling this in the best way possible. (You look from me to Simon.) Both of you agreed to this.

I am laughing harder now, and I snort once.

You: (to me) What? What is funny?

The Lovers Set Down Their Spoons

Me: (blowing my nose in my napkin and looking at you) You are funny. I am laughing at you.

The lover: (appearing behind the woman with whom you had an affair.) Have you seen a pair of glasses?

The four of us look up at him.

You: What the hell is going on here?

The lover: (to you) Look, buddy, I'm just looking for my reading glasses. I thought I left them on my table, but they're not there.

Me: (to the lover) Where is your—

The lover: She's out there (he points to the door) waiting for me. Just forgot my glasses—that's all. Anyway, I'm sorry. I didn't mean to interrupt.

Me: Oh. (To you) I was just about to say that I'm not going to be with you anymore.

You: (pointing to the woman with whom you had an affair) Because of her?

The woman with whom you had an affair: (opens her mouth slightly, as if she might say something, but then closes it and slowly reaches for her coffee cup).

You: (to me) Come on, you don't mean it. You're just upset.

Me: But I'm not upset. I've been upset for three years and I'm not anymore.

You: What are you talking about you've been upset for three years? I only saw her (again, pointing to the woman with whom you had an affair) for six months.

Simon: (to the woman with whom you had an affair) Six? (He looks from her, to you, then back to her.) You mean you two didn't get your story straight before our big night?

The woman with whom you had an affair: (reaches into her purse and pretends she is looking for something very important).

Simon: (to me) You want to split a cab?

Me: No. Thanks.

Simon stands up.

Me: (to Simon) But I'll walk out with you.

You: (to Simon and me) I knew it—I knew it all along. I knew you two were seeing each other.

Simon starts for the door, the lover follows him and I follow the lover.

Me: (to the lover as we step into the night) But I don't see your—

The lover: She's holding a cab somewhere…(he scans the curb). There she is—see?

The lover's lover is pushing against the grill of a taxi to keep it from moving forward. The driver is yelling and swearing out his rolled-down window.

The lover's lover: (calling from the street) Are you ready, my love?

The lover: (to Simon and me) Well, looks like we're off.

The lovers disappear into the yellow of the taxi, and the taxi (huffing and puffing and chugging along) disappears into the side mirrors of other taxis.

Me: (to Simon, when we can no longer see the lovers) It was a pleasure meeting you.

Simon: And you.

I take a step backwards and a crunch! erupts from under my foot.

Simon: What was that?

The Lovers Set Down Their Spoons

Me: (quickly) Nothing.

Simon: You stepped on something. I heard it.

Me: I'm afraid to look. I know what it is.

Simon: (bending down to the pavement, he picks up the lover's glasses.) You snapped off the right arm.

Me: (reaching for the glasses, holding them up to the streetlight) The lenses aren't cracked. (I look more closely.) There's not even a scratch. (I fold the left arm and carefully place the glasses inside my coat pocket.) I should get these to him. He probably can't read without them. Where do you think they went?

Simon: I don't know where lovers go.

Me: (stepping backwards toward the restaurant) I'll check inside. He might have left his information with the host. Maybe I can catch him before they've gone too far.

Simon: (handing me the broken arm) You should take this.

Me: Thanks. Well. I guess this is goodnight.

Simon: Goodnight.

After a brief handshake, I watch Simon walk down the street becoming smaller and smaller before getting into a cab. I reach into my pocket and pull out the glasses. I set them on my nose and fit the left arm behind my ear. Hazy shapes begin fusing and breaking apart, like organisms on a microscope slide. My eyes focus and the images sharpen. Then: clarity. The world stops. The streetlights turn red. And the moon, as you would expect, is enormous.

Jen Karetnick

The Eff Off Villain Elles

1. Dirty Laundry

It huddles protectively in the bins,
hiding weeks of history, telling lies.
Do you see how it layers like intestines?

It's time to ruin a new bottle of Gain,
cover my losses with odors that please,
that fold innocuously into the bins,

permit the epic flood of evidence:
who fights; who cheats; who, at night, still pees.
Do you see how it twists like intestines?

Time again for those color separations,
clothing apartheid, delicate whites that see
Spray 'n' Wash favors while still in the bins.

And time also for the cycles of pain,
the tumbling abuse of bras and panties.
See? They knot and resist like intestines,

bear stains that refuse definition,
and none of these machines offer release.
Laundry lies, in wait, in the bins.
I feel it digesting me, like intestines.

THE EFF OFF VILLAIN ELLES

2. Supernumerary Nipple

This is the mistake some genes still make:
an appendix, a coccyx, an extra teat.
For this I would have burned at the stake.

Vestigial? No, I was a modern freak,
afraid to show my flat chest in a two-piece suit.
This is the mistake some genes still make—

I was told it's a freckle, a birthmark.
But with that slit nubbin, how not to suspect?
For this I would have burned at the stake,

witch and familiar in the same hot dark;
now in the fall of breast, you can't see it.
Still, here's a mistake the genes still make:

The third nipple, unwanted, lets down milk
while two others, regulation-size, await.
For this I should be burned at the stake

yet I put the baby's lips to where the fit is exact.
Renounce me. I forgive you. You'll forget.
This is the mistake some genes still make.
For this, I refuse to burn at the stake.

3. To Menses

It's not enough to say I've had it with you.
Others so afflicted feel the same:
The womb, that abacus, subtracts its due.

An unwilling accomplice, I sweat to
shoot you from the hard drive of cell and meme.
It's not enough to say I've had it with you;

pre-programmed, I can't quit until you do,
playing your eternal numbers game.
The womb, that abacus, subtracts its due,

but recall, I've contributed funds, too,
nurturing them in this bank—the very same.
It's not enough to say I've had it with you

or even fair, as there have been dividends: two
(though they have grown up to deposit blame.)
The womb, that abacus, subtracts its due.

Am I really to be finished with its use,
and share no longer in this work of shame?
It's time enough to say I've had it with you.
The womb, that abacus, says my account is due.

4. *To Melasma*

I never was a pretty girl but I got by
on my legs (let's be honest), my turns of phrase,
and my skin, which had something young to say.

Now it's another sun blossoming every day.
Go ahead, disfigure me, make me so conscious
of how I can't be a pretty girl, can't get by

without cosmetics to misdirect the eye
the way metaphors conceal the same old clichés.
But so muted, I don't know what to say.

Understand, I'm not looking for advice;
I know you're immune equally to creams and pleas.
I never was a pretty girl but I got by

The Eff Off Villain Elles

until this mask you left me from pregnancy
and exposure to the climate I chose.
An age spot only has so much to say.

Well, fuck it. I'll take these patches as beauty,
highlight my cheekbones with their wise shadows.
I never was a pretty girl but I got by.
And now, at least, I have something to say.

Note: only sections two through four of this poem were entered in The Knightville Poetry Contest contest per our 70-line contest rule; here printed in full.

Michael Pearce

Tattoo

Let's just say it's who you were when you got it,
that day you went to the little shop at 6th and Mission
sharing a blunt with your skinny squeeze Kuff
and the jacket you had on was too warm in the sun
but that jacket wasn't about comfort anyway and anyway it was
just you and Kuff marching into a fateful afternoon
and the sign said parlour with a u and in you walked and there you were
face to face with a grisly grinning guy who wanted your business.

So who were you? A smart girl who'd quit school
and hung with Kuff and Wren and Bobby and Bobby's yappy pup Roo
and read more than they did and liked the music they played
and got high almost every day and tried to believe them
when they said today is today and tomorrow isn't anything
until it's today, and you were the same girl who'd go find a payphone
that worked and call up your dad and argue with him for an hour
until you both gave up one more time.

Let's just say you look at it now wrapped like a vine
around your neck and breasts and it's got some of the blur and bleed of memory
but none of that brutal loss that can wipe out a week or a person for years
until a dog's bark or peestink alley spits them back up at you,
and you don't enjoy looking at sad wan colors
but it is a slice of who you were when it happened and you know
you need to remember that: Kuff's bearded cheek on the blue pillow
on the mattress on the floor of that big apartment full of long lost compadres.

Tattoo

Pick a day any day today for instance you're standing in a schoolroom
watching your willful seven-year-old watch a chick hatch
and your brain doesn't know but your body does that this is
day 3000 in the new life you chose even before the shuddering moment,
and your body knows some other things, but it's not telling, not today,
it doesn't have the words or the pictures or the appetite,
and all you have left to remember this, now, is hiding,
is needling your thick skin from the inside.

Matt Miller

Asante

—after Allen Ginsberg's *America*

Asante, you dropped the ball.
Asante, you son of a bitch.
An interception would have ended
the drive, saved us from the helmet catch,
the loss, the upset.
Asante, I keep seeing it in my dreams.
Asante, I needed that win.
Asante, my brothers needed it. My mother.
Asante, my father in his lucky shirt watched every game
that season, died the day after
you won the divisional playoffs against Jacksonville.
Asante, we watched him dying as we watched the game
we were supposed to go to on the hospital television.
Asante, when the paramedics came to his house
they tore open his lucky shirt and when he was revived
he was pissed off you should have seen how skinny
his anger had become eating through that tube
threaded into his gut that burned his skin in bile.
Asante, we watched him breathe to death.
Asante, you held out for more money.
Did that dropped ball have something to do
with the missed practices? Did you get paid enough?
Asante, the NFL is America.
Asante, the NFL is a beautiful high-class hooker.
She takes all my money but shows me a good time.
Asante, ticket prices went up again.
Asante, I paid for you to drop the ball.
Asante, my father got season tickets in 1981 when nobody
wanted to go and pissed-off fans threw grills on the field.
Asante, I am the NFL. I fucked myself with my fantasy team.

Asante

Asante, my father taught me fatherhood teaching me to catch
a football bulleted between the trees in the Ashby woods.
I bounced off the trees. Asante, "It hurts more when you drop it, eh?"
said a smile and a cigarette and a bright sun through the pines.
Asante, he could throw a ball so hard you should have seen it.
Asante, he was left handed except when he wrote.
Asante, I joked it was a good thing he died because that game
would have killed him. Asante, did you know that Eli
is the Hebrew word for God? Asante, Asante, lama sabachthani?
Asante, I could not sleep for months without seeing
replay replay replay of the ball bouncing off your hands.
Asante, there should have been something I could have done.

Should I have made them stop? Hook the ventilator back up?
Would he have gotten better? Asante, he was not getting better.
Asante, he told a friend but not his sons he was sick of fighting.
Asante, I went to my first game when I was eight. My dad
took us and my brother got yelled at by someone behind us
for getting up too often to go get food.
Asante, we were all thin then but my father.
Asante, you are just a number. Asante, my father was a handsome man.
Asante, I figured out the dream had nothing to do with you.
Asante, I figured it out minutes before I watched my wife's
grandmother—102!—breathe herself to death her lips pulled back
like my dad's did you know I was the last
one to leave the hospital room? As I left two kids
tried to come in, they had the wrong room, my dad
would have laughed his unthreading lungs off
to have seen them scared shitless by his withered corpse.
Asante, I think my mom needed it to be over
but she would never say so.
Asante, this is poetry you will never read it.
Asante, I am profiling. I played football too.
Asante, did you know your name comes from the Ashanti
of western Africa? Do you know about the Golden Stool?

Matt Miller

Is your soul safe? Asante, my father couldn't sit on a toilet
without shitting razorblades. Asante, do you trace your lineage
through your mother? My mother's father played
for the Green Bay Packers. Asante, I am a poet.
Asante, I am through with your nightmare.
Asante, my son is crying I have to go.

Note: NFL Defensive Back Asante Samuel dropped a possible interception of a pass by New York Giant's quarterback Eli Manning that would have secured a win in Super Bowl XLII as well as an undefeated season for Samuel's team, the New England Patriots.

J. Preston Witt

COLDBROOK

THE MOON WAS BRIGHT AND shone through a single hole onto Louie's eyelids, waking him up. The smell of blood and split intestines steamed about his nostrils. His thumb and middle finger were broken on each hand, and he could feel the bones pressing against the inside of his skin.

He tried to stand, but a two-by-four strapped to his back and running the entire length of his spine prevented him. He struggled to his feet, for a moment, but his back wasn't strong enough to stay hunched in the position that the two-by-four required, and he fell forward onto his mutilated hands. He would've screamed, but a pinecone had been duct-taped into his mouth. The howl of pain stayed in his head with nowhere to go.

The only tolerable position the bear getup allowed

was on his back so he rolled over. He'd first have to find out where he was—no, he knew where he was. He was in his own woods inside a rotting bear carcass. Pieces of the pinecone dislodged from their axis and threatened to choke him. He swallowed the bits he could manage.

His head pounded. He'd awakened as they were sewing the bear's stomach, and Hassner had promptly hit him in the head with the butt of a rifle, again—the third time that day. He kept track of things like that. Louie remembered hoping that he was dead right before going unconscious.

He had to think, had to figure out how they'd gotten him into this thing so that he could get himself out. His arms were covered in what he assumed was carpenter's cement—probably from his own tool bench. It stuck in spots and was definitely uncomfortable, but it hadn't worked like they'd intended. The bear was still too fresh, the skin too wet for the cement to adhere. Every inch of his body felt moist and slick. He was naked except for his underwear and they too were soaked with fluids from the bear's insides. The duct tape forced him to breathe out of his nose, which was as much torture as anything else.

They'd left some meat on the bear, he noticed, and filled the empty spaces around his bare legs and chest with what felt like heavy cattle rope, although he couldn't tell for certain. What were really holding him in place though were the stitches. They'd sewn up the bear's underbelly, and stitched him to the bear. Tens of tight fishing wire stitches ran down his arms and legs. It must've taken hours to do all this to him.

Hal had given him the bear, all right, and probably found himself pretty clever as well. Not given—loaned. Some bear meat they might give away. Worth the joke, so to speak. Not the head though and not the hide. Too valuable. And by the time they'd hunted the bear and Louie all over again, the hide would be nothing short of a treasure.

He needed to get moving. He rolled over onto his knees and rested his hands down but the second he applied any weight, the pain, the feeling of his snapped, jagged metatarsals threatening to protrude from his skin, overwhelmed him. He lay back down.

His hands were useless. They wouldn't recover from this. Somehow that realization didn't bother him as much as not being able to stand up straight. He couldn't think with his nose in the dirt. If he could just find a way to get himself onto his feet, he'd be fine. Then again, he wouldn't be able to see where he was walking even if he did manage to stand. His only vision of the outside world was through the bullet hole in the side of the animal's neck. Navigating the forest was going to be a chore. Hal had, obviously, not wanted him to get too far away.

The bear's head was above his own and flopped loosely side to side. Congealed blood—either his own or the bears—stuck to his face and itched. The itch was more distracting right then than the forty stitches or his pounding head or his broken fingers. He needed to think, and he needed to relax in order to think. He needed to—to look at the moon.

He spun himself on the ground to get a better angle at the sky, jostling the bear head to set the bullet hole in line with the opening in the forest ceiling. As he did this, the two-by-four strapped to his back shifted. Hardly, but it did move and now wasn't completely centered along his spine. He kicked at the earth and continued to spin, forgetting the moon and his original purpose for the awkward, flailing maneuver. The ropes that held the board in place dug into the skin around his midsection, but he kept at it.

The board finally shifted enough to allow him to stand. He still had to hunch, his balance tilted dangerously forward, but he was on his feet. The bear's skin was tight and loose in the wrong spots and shortened his stride even though the bear dwarfed him. He leaned up against a thin sapling for support.

He tested walking, a few steps, then leaned against the next closest sapling to steady himself. He shuffled to the next sapling, then the next, then the next.

He started to pick up speed, blind speed, moving from tree to tree, accidentally snapping a thin sapling in half as he stumbled along through the forest, his forest—he hoped it was his forest. His mind went to Emmett for a moment, whittling alone by the stove. Shipped off to some old uncle's house by his parents for the summer. Louie and his wife hadn't wanted children.

Louie knocked against a larger tree but without slowing, tearing his way through tangles of thorn-grass and nettles. He built up a great deal of momentum, a dragging force that propelled him forward through the warren of trees. He could feel the burs and branches gathering on the fur as he rebounded from sapling to tree to boulder, bouncing down the side of the gulley like a ball in a carnival peg maze, a gulley that, if he was on his land like he hoped, would eventually lead to an open field or to the road marking his property line.

At some point, he'd let go, quit pedaling—the pace being too fast for him—and he floated a few steps removed from his body. He watched himself stagger onward. He began to anticipate the collisions, to expect the surprises that the gauntlet of branches and trees threw at him. Gave up looking out of the almost useless hole in the side of the bear's neck and took the violent, painful dance in rhythm. Every inch of his body would be bruised and cut and broken when he stopped but as long as the thrust was at his back he let it carry him.

He doubted now as to whether the ground was declining or if he was being tricked by the leaning position the bear forced him to assume. Hours seemed to pass by in a daze, a muddle of confrontation. He was running blindfold through an oncoming Manhattan crowd. He was skiing through slalom gates. He was eight and his older brother was nudging him into telephone poles while riding his bike.

The bear's thick hide protected him from many of the thorns, branches and broken limbs that snagged at the fur instead of his own skin. His hands had grown numb from the wraps that attached them to the paws. The wrappings were far too tight and there was no way of knowing what his hands would look like once he freed himself from the bear hide. For now the numbness was a blessing. As Louie's mind gently drifted towards what would happen to his hands, he tripped over a root and fell face first into a fallen tree.

This was the first time he'd stopped moving in how long he didn't know. The blood pumped noisily in his chest and thighs and eardrums. The stitches on his right leg had all ripped free from the hide when he'd fallen—his skin wasn't as tough as the bear's. The blood ran freely, pooling into the bear's foot. After a few moments rest, he crawled his way underneath the downed tree.

He'd crawled a few yards when his knees came upon soft grass as opposed to the crunch of dry needles and twigs blanketing the forest floor. He peered out the bullet hole. The clearing he'd come across looked like it would lead out of the woods and onto the land behind his house. Either he'd circled the entire way around the property, a good five miles, or Hal had left him somewhere far south of his property line.

He lay down to rest for a moment more and positioned the bullet hole so that he could see the evening sky. There was no artificial light anywhere, but the night was hardly serene. The pain throbbing in his head, the adrenaline of the descent, the amount of active noise from the crickets and other wildlife all made the darkness seem inappropriate. Louie felt himself dozing off and stared directly at the moon to keep himself awake.

 Hal wouldn't hurt the boy. He'd too much pride to do a thing like that. Louie deserved it—well, not this, he didn't deserve this, nobody deserved this, but it was at least within the proper realm. Touching the boy on the other hand…

Although he knew Emmett had to be all right, he couldn't help imagining the boy, lost, wandering the ridge in his own bear suit.

Grey thin clouds (canoes) moved across the dark sky (a river) passing in front of the moon (the moon) and disappeared over the mass of dark forest in the distance (a waterfall). Frances was there lying in the field next to him. She was pale but glowed warm like the moon. I'm sorry I didn't fix the house, he said. I'm sorry. Frances only smiled.

A coyote howled from on top the hill to his right. Another joined in. And another answered. The coyotes weren't close by, but their voices in the dark made

Louie aware that he wasn't alone. He'd felt isolated as he bumbled through the woods in his bear suit. He was lucky not to have been found by any coyotes. Coyotes weren't good company. He'd be easy prey although they didn't normally go after humans. Or bears. Unless they were old and lame, that is.

With a new sense of urgency he forced himself to his feet and aimed for the road or his house. Whatever he stumbled upon first.

A coyote howled. Another joined in. And another answered.

Emmett sat inside by the fire with the rifle across his lap. Louie hadn't come home after going into town. The old man frequently took off for the woods or the creek or town without so much as a word, and Emmett had learned early on in the summer not to concern himself with where Louie was.

Although he usually was home by nightfall, this wasn't the first time Louie had left him alone for the night. Two weeks ago he went into town and didn't show up again until 9 a.m. the next day, smelling horribly of vodka when he did.

Even with Louie there, Emmett had a hard time sleeping in the house. The wind whistled through the rafters and up through the floor. Not to mention the mice that scuttled about as soon as it got quiet. Ridding the place of mice was Emmett's latest project and his plan was working—sort of. The problem was that the poison he used was unorthodox and slow acting. Louie had canned his own baked beans a couple years ago and the results were, literally, deadly. He'd screwed up one batch and the growth of a toxin in the beans created a gas inside the can, which expanded and caused those cans to be grossly misshapen. The bulges made the cans easy enough to avoid (for dinner) or to find (if there was something you wanted dead). Louie had given him the idea for using the beans.

"Botulism," Louie had said, "causes full-body paralysis by day three in humans. We thought your grandmother had it once when she was a girl." Paralyzed mice were hidden around the house like Easter eggs.

A scream—a deathly high-pitched shriek made Emmett nearly fall over in the armchair. Something was angry or dying. He jumped up and shut the three doors that led to the living room. He could watch all three easily from where he sat.

It shrieked again. He thought he'd be alright if he just holed up where he was, but it kept on, the desperate tone making him more and more tense. The strain of expectation from one cry to the next was almost unbearable, each new outburst causing him to jump violently. Although Emmett knew in his gut that a young woman was being eaten at that very moment by something vicious, he convinced himself that it must be an animal.

Emmett couldn't even discern from what direction the cry was coming from. He thought it was running around the outside, but at the same time the shrieks resonated throughout the house's many wooden rooms and hallways, making it sound far too close.

Until this summer, he never would've left the living room. The land and this house had forced him to become curious about simple things like where a creek began, how to skin a deer, how a transmission worked—what made death noises in the middle of the night and how to get it out of the house. He most likely wasn't in any real danger. He knew that, and he also knew that he could've waited out the screams if need be. But he wanted the screaming stopped. It's what Louie would've done if he was home.

Emmett's resolve hardened. He listened. He'd thought the scream was upstairs, but as soon as he crept up the stairwell, rifle at the ready, it sounded again. This time from downstairs in the workroom. Storming back down the steps, trying to make as much noise as possible, he came to the entrance.

He checked that the breech was closed and the safety, off, then stepped inside, pointed the flashlight into the far corner, into the near corner. Moving tentatively into the room, he shined the light at a flat wheelbarrow tire and at the stack of hubcaps against the wall.

It screamed. Then something else off to his right screamed. There were two. One of them was outside. And nothing was in the workroom. Terrified as he was, Emmett had to admit the thrill of the decrepit house in the middle of nowhere, the rifle in his hand, the firelight, and the midnight mystery of the whole event. All this had slightly intoxicated him.

There was a scratching noise he hadn't heard earlier, and he followed the noise to the room with the shut door at the back of the house. He didn't know how it could've gotten in there. The door was stuck and Emmett had to kick its base to open it. He readjusted the rifle to under his arm cowboy style before entering.

The room with the shut door was the only renovated room in the house. The walls were a delicate purple. The trim, carefully detailed, each intricate carving sanded clean by hand, then stained rich and dark. Emmett scanned the floor with the flashlight looking for it. The floor felt sturdy under his feet unlike most of the other rooms where Emmett was always prepared to catch himself should he fall through. Louie never used the room. Hated it in fact. Kept the door shut. Said it reminded him of a dump in Greenwich Village he'd stayed in once and if he wanted to live in Manhattan, he'd live in Manhattan for Chrissake—the old man had a point. No reason to fix a place to look like home. Might as well stay at home.

It screamed directly behind him. Emmett screamed back, juggled the rifle and the flashlight, which fell to the floor. The light on the floor revealed two eyes no more than a few yards in front of him. It screamed again and Emmett screamed again and he pointed the rifle and fired. The echo from the shot rang in his ears for a good minute. He waited until his head quieted down then retrieved the flashlight from the floor and pointed it at where the eyes had been.

A baby raccoon no larger than a puppy had taken the bullet in the side. It was the first thing Emmett had ever killed. A baby raccoon was nothing to brag about though. Still shook up, Emmett decided to leave the raccoon for the morning when he could dispose of it properly and, closing the door behind him, went from the room. Louie would make him skin and eat it if he found out. He'd bury it behind the woodshed where Louie wouldn't notice.

He sat back down in the armchair in front of the stove. With the gun securely on his lap, the fire he'd started burning with the wood he'd chopped, the raccoon he'd shot resting in peace in the back room—his fear drifted away. He breathed easy, felt confident and able to relax for the first time since the sun went down.

Moving from the stove, he went out to the porch where a stiff-backed wooden chair rested against the side of the house. The moon was bright and washed the clouds as they drifted by.

The house on the other hand was filthy. He sniffed his shirt. He was filthy. That fit. Somehow it was the point of being here in the first place. Louie never cleaned or repaired anything unless it was absolutely necessary. The room with the shut door said that well enough—pretty, purple, and unused.

There was another scream, but it was low-pitched now and farther away. His throat tightened. A baby raccoon. A careening mother. He tried to shake the thought, but it wouldn't leave. He shook his head, forcefully—his skull a rattle and his thoughts the little beads or whatever the hell's inside a rattle, he didn't know.

Emmett noticed movement in the distance off to the left, which then disappeared into the thick mist that covered the field. He could hear feet shuffling down the dirt road toward the house. The momentary panic of the strange and unknown moving about in the dark quickly subsided. The outline of the figure came into view, then stumbled off the road and into the grass, out of sight. It was Louie, and he was drunk again by the way he was walking. Emmett got up from the chair.

He didn't blame Louie for drinking. Emmett's own father never drank and was a righteous ass because of it, in Emmett's opinion. The family would've been much better off and his parents probably wouldn't be divorcing right now if more people had taken more drinks at his house. It's sometimes easier to forgive a drunk.

Then again, if they hadn't been divorcing he wouldn't have gotten out of the Christian sports camp. He'd spent every summer he could remember inside a football helmet. It was thanks to Louie, really, that he wasn't in a bunk room full of fifty sweaty guys—Louie had convinced his father that he'd work him hard, keep him in shape, and teach him a few things in the meantime. Emmett enjoyed football but compared to shooting raccoons and using an axe and a hammer and building benches and fires and gutting animals, football felt sterile, like a substitute for the real thing. He might consider not playing football in the fall. Depending on how much he wanted to piss off his father.

He waited for Louie to reappear. After a few minutes had passed, Emmett began to think the old man had fallen over and gone to sleep. Emmett chuckled to himself and headed out to the road to fetch him for bed. Louie had made it a hundred or so yards from the house. The moon lit things well enough, but Emmett brought the rifle along anyway. It'd become a comfort to him and the closest thing he'd had to a teddy bear in some time. He glanced back and noticed that the house seemed warm and inviting at the moment with the firelight glowing inside.

When Emmett came to the road, he could hear harsh, troubled breathing. Worried, he quickened his step until he got to where he'd seen Louie fall over. A potent unrecognizable smell—like rotten mayonnaise or aged fish, maybe—hung about the humid air, and he took to breathing through his shirt sleeve. He hoped that smell wasn't coming from Louie. Their beds were next to each other.

The field mist was thick, obscuring his vision to only a few feet now that he was out walking around in it.

"Louie?" he said, quietly, attempting to prevent something other than Louie from answering.

As if in response, a figure rose slowly above the grass line with a great deal of effort. It was much larger than Louie. It wasn't human. It couldn't be. The figure moved forward into the moonlight revealing a black bear reared up on its hind legs. It stood within a few yards of him.

The bear didn't make a noise, but stared directly at him for a moment, mouth agape, then turned to look at something across the road. Even through the haze of thick mist, it didn't look right to him. Not that he'd ever seen one in person, to be fair, but it looked sick, its head oddly contorted, its skin sagging—something from a bad horror movie.

Emmett switched the safety off. The bear reacted to the soft click of the lever and began clawing at the air with its front paws, still balancing on its hind legs. Emmett aimed the rifle at its head and waited for it to make a move. It dropped down to all fours. He wanted it to run away, wanted to tell it to get lost, but thinking about that frightened him even more. Bears don't listen to 'No' or 'Stop' or even feel bad when they're eating your face.

He didn't know how many shots it took to kill a bear and didn't care to find out. And at the same time, from the little corner in his brain that'd appreciated the neatly chopped wood and the fire and the raccoon, came a brief fantasy about what Louie would say if he got a bear all on his own. He could even see Louie's face, could see him bragging to Hal about the whole affair on his behalf. The thought sat there in the back of his skull.

Louie had told him what to do if he'd ever come across a bear. You weren't to run away or show fear. Even a few steps backwards could be trouble. Emmett held his ground with his finger resting on the trigger.

The bear's head appeared above the grass line. It wasn't looking in his direction but across the road again. At what, Emmett couldn't see. Bears sense of smell was something like seven times better than a bloodhound, but it'd reacted to him as if it'd been surprised at his presence. It hadn't run away, or attacked, or even warned him with anything more than a small, sickly growl. Emmett resisted removing his hands from the rifle to cover his nose: the bear smelled worse than fifty wet dogs.

It stared across the road for a good while, hardly moving. If he just hit it a few times in the chest, right behind the front leg where the heart was supposed to be, it'd go down. It'd have to. And that'd be it. He could actually do this, he thought. The bear was old or sick or both and didn't appear at all aggressive. An easy target.

Emmett aimed the rifle.

The bear threw itself up onto its hind legs, let out a soft gurgling growl and took two swift steps in Emmett's direction. Emmett fired.

It dropped down, but kept advancing.

Emmett cleared the breech, loaded, and fired again.

The round hit the bear in the chest. It faltered and fell to all fours, but was still moving.

Emmett cleared the breech, loaded the chamber, paused, and fired.

The bear groaned and stopped.

Emmett ejected the empty cartridge, reloaded and, to be sure, fired again. Nothing, not a flinch.

He shouted just once at the dead bear in an outburst of excitement. Emmett could already see himself holding the tanned hide and telling the story to a room of men wanting to buy him drinks and cigars.

He paused, now faced with having to touch it with his hands. He'd have to get it into the woodshed, protected from other wildlife and off of the ground by the time Louie returned. Emmett could feel the little bubble of fear in his head start to grow again, but he shook it out. Not taking proper care of the bear meat was the kind of thing that'd make his uncle livid. And an angry Louie was at least as frightening as a bear. He nudged the bear with his foot and leapt backwards to safer ground. Nothing, not a flinch.

Louie would've probably cut the bear apart right there, solving the problem, but Emmett wasn't up for tearing a bloody animal's insides out. Not in the middle of the night, not by himself. Emmett's nerve wasn't hard enough. That was the difference between him and Louie.

Groping a dead bear at midnight without his rifle close by made him anxious to get back to the fire. Emmett felt his courage dwindling quickly. The bear was heavy but the long grass was wet with dew and allowed it to slide with relative ease all the way into the woodshed. Hal had lectured him about hanging a deer with the head facing downward and from a specific leg joint. But Emmett had watched his uncle hang a fawn by the neck just yesterday. He'd better do it Louie's way.

The chain was on a simple lock-pulley system, and Emmett looped it around the bear's neck and secured the clasp. The bear was hoisted up. After a few moments a stream of fluid ran off one of the bear's hind legs. The smell overpowered him. He left, shut the woodshed door, and jogged back to the armchair by the fire.

The smell clung to his hands and his shirt. He tore off his shirt and washed it in the bucket of creek water he'd filled earlier that day. The water was warm from resting against the stove.

Only a few coals remained in the fire. He added another log and blew on the embers until the fire was going well enough to last the night. Emmett lay down in the cot stretched across the wall nearest the stove, warmed by wood he'd split burning in a fire he'd started.

Michael Bazzett

Odds

I've been alive for sixteen thousand and ninety days
which means that in sixteen thousand and eighty-nine
of those days I have not been in an accident where I
felt the car fishtail into a glide looked at my wife uttered
fuck in the most feeling sense of that ancient syllable
felt our little wagon slam nose-first into concrete
hood flailing back like a broken wing catastrophic noise air
bag snapping my head back cleanly splitting my nose while
we spun in holiday traffic and honking cars wove around us
like a hurtling school of tuna until we crept to a stop and I
stood outside the crumpled rear door jerking a broken
handle the screaming face of my son registering no sound.

On sixteen thousand and eighty-nine of those days I did
not sit unplanned broken stunned on the rainy shoulder
of a Minnesota road gravel smelling of iron not feeling
anything words knocked clear a perfect blankness.

On sixteen thousand and eighty-nine of those days I didn't
lose my virginity in anxious sweat break my neck put my dog
down feel the jolt of earth come up through my bended knee
see my daughter come wide-eyed to the world see my son
come bull-shouldered I didn't search for a pulse in the small
bones of my grandfather's wrist and call my mother to say
I'd held his hand as he'd died. On sixteen thousand and
eighty-nine of those days I did not make the decision to sit
here and write this all down nor did the decision make me.
It didn't happen. Then it did and not because of some line
etched across my nose or the fused ribs inside my wife or
the surprisingly large feathered cask of the bald eagle's body
perched in the oak this morning when I walked with my son
and he pointed up and exclaimed and I could hear every word.

Hal LaCroix

The Numbers

Wear and tear identify us, lines drawn

by accident, love and abuse.

Francisco (Frank) Munoz who fell on 9/11

had three identifying marks

according to his wife's pasted-up flyer:

> 1) left index finger does not extend,
> 2) scar above right eye,
> 3) brown birthmark

splashed on his back. Locate all three

and you've got Frank, not some other guy

with just, say, one mark, the brown splash

or two marks, the scar and the bent-crooked finger

for itching the scar, for calling loved ones.

Yet. Is no other man on this tilted Earth crafted

in this triple way? I got to wondering

what are the chances. So I ran the numbers

and found 55 million men whose left index fingers

The Numbers

do not extend and 398 million with scars

above right eyes and regarding birthmarks on backs

67,000 present themselves as brown and splashed

and it took a supercomputer in Osaka, Japan

to chop the total down to 14 men marked by

the three stigmata of Francisco (Frank) Munoz.

One fell that day.

Kevin Carollo

Collateral

> *Our heavy hearts still hold the hope that we can restore inside our country the acknowledgement of your humanity that we were taught to deny.* —Ethan McCord and Josh Steiber, in an open letter to the people of New Baghdad neighborhood

You are just as guilty   as the soldier
pulling the trigger.   Mirror, you are the
drill sergeant telling   the cadet to get the
sand out of his vagina.   But perhaps we are
all vaginas after a fashion,   vague open letters
of humanity whose very life-   giving beauty and
potential we have in   plentiful abundance but
have always been   taught to deny. Perhaps the
cradle of civilization   is a heady euphemism for
the holy egg and jism   incubated in a glorious
Original Vagina in a   hot and fertile land
formerly going by the   frankly labial name of
Mesopotamia.   Mesopotamia,
as if this wild and new   flavor of human ice
cream, this seemingly   predestined maelstrom
of beauty and potential,   would be licked and
licked with reckless love   and abandon for a good
millennium at least, if   not more, down to the
very delta-like depths   of the cone. But our
heavy hearts knew   this not even close
was just what was   in the cards. We knew
who got left with   the short bone of a half-
wish. We went far   away, settled on the
readiest euphemisms,   if not the most
apt. Our bodies were   ossuaries of unknown
soldiers firing into   crowds in a hundred
years war with each   blind new day. My dear

Collateral

fellow vaginas, I don't know where to stick
or store this war. I don't know what to do
with remote control. Throughout all of
recorded history, in fact, people have been
called upon to put up their own children as
a form of collateral. The list is endless, and
it is getting late. I don't have the exact specifics,
something something we are less and less safe
something end stop. We are labile but able
bodies. We just won't ever know what we
are wont to. We are gathered here today.

Jaed Coffin

The Nice Guy

THE FIRST MAN I EVER FOUGHT was a Haida Indian twice my age who looked partly white and whose name was Mike "The Nice Guy" Edenshaw. At the time, I was twenty-one years old and one year out of college back east. The Nice Guy was forty-two and worked as a janitor at a nursing home. He is dead now.

We fought on a snowy Friday night in late November, in a twenty-foot-by-twenty-foot boxing ring, in a barroom above a diner called Donna's. The name of the bar was Marlintini's Lounge and on Friday nights during the winter months men from the capital city and from the smaller towns and fishing villages along the Inside Passage like Cordova, Yakutat, Angoon, Klawock, and Hoonah came to Marlintini's to fight each other in the Roughhouse Friday boxing shows. For the seven years that I trained as

The Nice Guy

a fighter, I only spent one year—my first—boxing in the Roughhouse show, but as far as I know, the show goes on.

The morning of the fight, I arrived in Juneau with my trainer, Victor Littlefield, on the 6 a.m. flight from Sitka—the small fishing town of eight thousand where I worked in a high school and trained in Victor's gym. Victor is a Tlingit Indian, whose family and clan have lived in Southeast Alaska for over ten thousand years. During the day, he works as an electrician at the local hospital; at night, he trains a small stable of young men from town. Victor has a son, and is married to a woman he has known his whole life. In his fighting days, he went by "The Savage."

The first time I walked into Victor's gym—this was early in October, after the cruise ships had all returned south and after the salmon had spawned and then died in the same rivers where they were born—Victor asked me if I wanted to fight him. I had never boxed before, but after paddling a sea kayak one thousand miles north from Seattle, I was in good enough shape to think I might win. Victor must have hit me fifty times in the first minute of our match. When he decided that I'd had enough, he invited me back to his gym to train full time. Single, brave, looking for something to care about, I started working out with Victor every Monday, Wednesday, and Friday night. Three weeks later, Victor asked me if I wanted to fly over to Juneau and fight someone in a bar. If I won, he said, a man was going to give me one hundred and fifty dollars. "It's no ballroom," Victor told me. "Basically, you just take your shirt off and show everyone how tough you are." And then Victor told me that I needed to have a ring name. We tried a few out—"Half Asian Sensation," "Thai Thunder"—until Victor suggested "The Stone," because it went well with my last name—Coffin—and because even though I got hit a lot, I never let on that it hurt.

It rained all morning in Juneau. Victor and I sat in Donna's eating biscuits and moose gravy while Victor told me stories of his fights. In the afternoon, we rented a car and drove all the way to the end of the Juneau road just to see it, and then into town to walk the aisles of a department store, and then we took a long nap and watched hunting shows in our room at the Travel Lodge—the hotel where the fight promoter had put us up across the street from Marlintini's. Night fell about four p.m. By six, the first heavy snow of the season began to fall. At eight o'clock, Victor told me it was time for us to go over.

I followed Victor across the street and upstairs to Marlintini's. At the door, Victor told the bouncers that I was his fighter, and the bouncers waved me through. The crowd—at capacity, Marlintini's could fit 400 people—had been drinking heavily since nine. You could hear the booze in the careless chatter that registered every time the music—AC/DC, Ja Rule and Nelly—cut out, and you could see the crowd's rising intoxication sparkling in the dim light. The majority of the fans were native—mostly Tlingit or Haida—or else they were Filipino, Mexican, Samoan, and white. They huddled around small ringside tables for which they'd paid thirty-five dollars per chair to sit at, or they stood, for twenty-five bucks, shoulder to shoulder, peering out from under baseball hats and dark hoodies. Back then, you could still smoke in bars in Alaska, and so lots of people did.

The other fighters were in the corner of the barroom, doing jumping jacks and throwing punches in the air, or jogging in place while slapping themselves in the face. Everyone was acting pissed off and ferocious, but you could tell that some of the guys who looked the angriest were the ones who were most afraid to fight. The women who had come to watch them were all dressed up for a big night out: visible thongs and lots of cleavage and bangs sprayed up into big claws that rose off their foreheads. Victor put our gear in a corner near the pool tables and we sat down against the wall. Through the crowd and smoke I could see the fight ring: the canvas spot-lit and blood-dappled, the ropes the colors of the American flag.

"You got any idea who I'm fighting tonight?" I asked Victor. For the last week, I'd been waking up several times each night to think about the man. In the darkness, he was always much bigger and meaner and stronger than me.

Victor looked at me from under the brim of his hat. He has dark eyes and white Chinese skin and a face that is round and supple like a seal's. Somewhere in the past, Victor once told me, there was Russian blood.

"It doesn't matter," Victor said. Then he got up and walked over to a small table where a large white woman with a clipboard sat and where earlier I'd had to sit, in a chair while an EMT with several lip rings gave me a physical exam that confirmed that I wasn't drunk and that I didn't have any broken bones.

"It's that old native dude," Victor said when he came back. The barroom was mostly full of "native dudes," but I knew exactly who Victor was talking about. The Nice Guy stood just beyond the pool tables, punching a cement pillar with one palm while sucking drags off another man's cigarette, which he cupped in his wrapped hand like a joint. His hair was long over his ears, he wore a heavy and untrimmed mustache, and his arms hung from his paddling shoulders with a sense

The Nice Guy

of defeat and unimportance.

"Anything else?" I said.

Victor shrugged. "Name is Mike Edenshaw. Calls himself 'The Nice Guy.'"

The Nice Guy, I thought. I liked The Stone better. "How many fights he got?"

Victor frowned and then looked at me squarely. He bobbed his head left under an imaginary right hand, and came up with a left cross of his own. We were both southpaws, and this was a move we'd been working on for the last several days. Victor called it his "sleep button." He'd hit me with a lot in the last weeks. "All I know is that if you slip his right and come up with a left," Victor said, "you'll knock his ass out."

About ten-thirty p.m., Victor sat me down in a backward metal chair and wrapped my hands. When he was done wrapping he slid on my gloves. In a quiet corner of the barroom, he took me through combinations hook-cross-hook. Cross-hook-cross. Pop-pop-pop. When I'd worked up a good sweat, I jogged in place watching the other fights. In the ring an old Tlingit man knocked out a teenaged black kid with an ugly and nearly accidental punch that sent the kid to the canvas, wiggling. Two obese fighters, after ten seconds of the first round, were stooped over, exhausted and panting, as the crowd booed for them to keep fighting. After one of the bikini-clad ring girls circled the barroom with a card that read ROUND 2, the more obese fighter got a bolt of life and knocked out the other man with a punch to the back of his head.

It was my turn to fight. Before I made my way to the ring, I kneeled in the corner and then whispered a short Buddhist prayer even though I didn't know what it meant. I stood up and walked behind Victor through the crowd and into my corner.

In the middle of the ring, barking into a microphone, stood a red-faced man in a derby hat, with a red-sequin tuxedo vest and a matching bowtie. The man was Bob Haag, the H of Big H Promotions and the mind behind Roughhouse Friday. At the time, Haag's show was the most successful entertainment event in all of Southeast, which meant that it beat out all the other monthly offerings at Marlintini's Lounge—a category which included a pole dancing cabaret of various local women, Salsa and Texas Hold 'Em nights, Sunday Afternoon Pajama Karaoke, and a touring group of Midget Wrestlers who stapled dollar bills to each other's heads.

"In the red corner, from a town called Ketchikan," Haag growled into his microphone, "he works as a night janitor at the Mountain View Senior Home…calls himself The Nice Guy…" The crowd, by then, was too drunk to cheer for anything but violence. And then: "He's a school teacher in Sitka, calls himself 'The Stone'!"

I jogged in my corner. Victor slapped my face with Vaseline and then offered me some final wisdom: "Crush skulls," he said. "Steal souls. You're a fucking warrior."

Ding. Ding. Ding.

Standing there across from The Nice Guy in the moments before either of us had thrown a punch, I encountered a kind of amplified silence unlike any silence I had ever heard before. A comparison might be drawn to a heightened state of meditation, but that was not exactly it. I mean yes there was the same electric sense of emptiness—elevated now by the vast whiteness of the blood-dappled canvas, and yes there was the same fuzzy murmur—this from the murmuring crowd, but the big difference between what happens in the mind and what happens in the ring is that rather than encountering the slow breath of my dissolving self, I instead found myself confronting, through the slim space between red leather gloves, the dark eyes of another man.

The Nice Guy did not move much, but rather stood mostly still, or shuffling, flat-footed, open-mouthed, as if waiting for me to come forward. When I threw the first punch, I did not do it out of aggression; I threw it because I wanted to end the abysmal silence that hung between me and my opponent.

It was just a meek jab, followed by a few more. Victor was yelling something from behind me, but I did not hear it. The crowd was growing unsatisfied. To please them, I kept moving forward and jabbing. The Nice Guy—hands low—refused to move. And then: bang.

The punch landed flush on my cheek. The crowd erupted, but it did not hurt. In fact, the slap of impact made me feel better, and it made me wake up to the fact that there, standing across from me, was a man with whom I probably had very little in common beyond the terms of our simple agreement: to punch each other.

Ding. Ding. Ding.

The Nice Guy

Between rounds, Victor took out my mouth guard and sponged my shoulders and face while telling me, "This guy's cold. He's fucking old. He's all dried up. Look at him." I was sitting on a stool in the blue corner, trying to slow my breathing. Victor had taken out my mouth guard and given me water then told me to spit it into a bucket. "He's fucking old, man," he said. "Be a warrior. Hit him. Run him. He won't last."

When I looked across the ring to where The Nice Guy was slumped over on a stool, I realized that Victor was right: his cheeks had turned a gray shade of yellow and the skin of his sagging chest was puckered and blushed. He stared at the mid-ceiling as though it were a pleasant afternoon sky. Maybe a sunset. There was not a drop of sweat on him.

In the next round, I came out fast. I threw big wild punches for about twenty seconds, and while none of them landed cleanly, the pressure and weight of them began to damage The Nice Guy's enthusiasm. At one point, we locked in an awkward clinch. The Nice Guy's head was stuck in my armpit, but Haag—who doubled as ref—let us fight on. So I started punching, clumsy uppercuts that landed on The Nice Guy's chin and throat. After I landed two or three—his head remained about waist high, the physics of our clinch seemed to trap it there, bobbing—something deep inside my stomach flexed, flashed, and broke loose. Whatever the feeling was, I had never felt it before and I knew that I was in no position to hold it back. When Haag broke us apart, I ran at The Nice Guy and punched him several more times. By now, I could feel the hardness of his skull through the padding in my gloves, and the dull sensation only made me want to find it again. Then I felt The Nice Guy's body bend, and sink. I backed off when he fell to his knees.

Ding. Ding. Ding.

By the time he rose for the third round, The Nice Guy's punches looped toward me at no more than quarter speed. As I slipped them, I could hear heavy, taxing breaths leave his chest. I was no boxer then—and I suppose that over time I still never became much more than a decent fighter—but The Nice Guy's slowness gave me that thrilling sensation of absolute control. Each time he swung, I ducked and countered with sleep-button left crosses followed by more right hooks—as if Victor and I had choreographed the sequences weeks ago.

The next time The Nice Guy threw a blind right hand, I slipped it and immediately felt the power building in my toe, traveling through my calf, my knee, rising into my hips and stomach, turning over in my shoulder. When the power reached my wrist, my fist could do nothing but snap.

Pop.

The Nice Guy went down. He wobbled to his feet and remained there unmoving. I drilled him again, harder, near his temple. Pop. This time, flat onto his back. His feet kicked up into the air—like an insect, or a cartoon of the just-dead—and for what seemed like too long, the feet remained there above him. Haag had already counted up to four; I stood in the neutral corner. The crowd erupted. I believe that I turned to the barroom and raised my arms. But it was while watching his feet rise, and then hang there, that I noticed the details of The Nice Guy's sneakers.

They were brand new basketball shoes, colored bright white and dazzle red. The shoes seemed comically adolescent for a forty-three year old man, and as The Nice Guy crawled across the canvas and dumbly pawed at the air, I found myself imagining him strolling down the aisle of the department store in Juneau, his hands in his pockets, a bashful look on his face, then stopping to admire the shoes, turning them over in his hands, fighting back a pang of giddiness, cursing the price tag, then telling himself: to hell with it, because tonight, as he moved beneath the golden spot light of Marlintini's, they were going to be worth every penny.

It took several minutes for The Nice Guy to come to. He went to his corner, where someone removed his gloves, and then he wandered to the middle of the ring. Meanwhile, Victor and I celebrated my first victory. The crowd liked what they saw—perhaps they hadn't seen much, but I was the product of an old champion, I was new, I had won, and they were drunk and someone had gotten knocked down and that was good enough reason to stand up and scream.

"Get up on the ropes!" Victor said. "Give them what they want!"

I put my feet on the middle rope, and rose up with my hands over my head. It was a stupid and arrogant gesture but I could not stop myself. In that moment—the crowd swelling beneath me, the ring alive and throbbing while winter and darkness and snow and cold hovered outside—I believed I would be the next middleweight champion of Roughhouse Friday, and I believed that winning that title would come with no irony or complexity and at no cost to me or anyone else.

The Nice Guy and I shook hands; our shake became an embrace. "Good fight," he said. His voice was much higher than I thought it would be, and his breath left his body in short wheezes. For the first time that night, I worried that he was not all right.

"Hey," I said, but I did not know what I was going to say next. "I wish...," I was looking at The Nice Guy's drawn face, which had suddenly become boyish and un-menacing. "I wish I could have fought you when you were my age."

The Nice Guy

The Nice Guy looked at me, turned his head sideways. My intention was to compliment him, but by the time I realized it had not come across this way it was too late.

"Oh," said The Nice Guy.

Haag raised my hand. The Nice Guy smiled to himself, took my other hand, and raised it also. As he exited the ring, one of his sneakers got snagged in the ropes. He stumbled into the crowd. Later, I tried to find The Nice Guy with the intention of buying him several beers with my winner's check, perhaps splitting a package of cigarettes, meeting the rest of the Edenshaw family. I spent several minutes searching the barroom for signs of his red track suit—but I guess he was already gone.

I did not stay in Alaska for very long. I fought Roughhouse for the rest of that year, and, after winning a middleweight title that spring in what Bob Haag called "The Southeast Showdown," I moved back east, to Maine. In Portland, I joined up with a top-level boxing club, with serious pro fighters and elite amateurs who fought in Golden Gloves tournaments all over the country. I never did tell my coach or the other fighters about my past in Alaska. For all I cared, fighting a bunch of Indians in a barroom didn't count for boxing experience. Over the next several years, I racked up enough amateur bouts to be deemed a respectable handful. I learned how to move and counter and adjust to different fighting styles in a way that Victor would never have been able to teach me. They were things one could learn only by leaving a remote place like Southeast.

And then one November, while training for a big regional tournament, my sparring partner—a lightning fisted middleweight from Haiti named Lamour—caught me with a jab I never saw. I did not black out, and the punch left me with no stitches. But for the next several weeks, I couldn't get rid of my headaches and nausea. I tried to run it off, but the symptoms wouldn't shake. MRIs and CT scans all negative, I returned to the gym with the intention of fighting again. But whenever I hit the heavy bag, or did a push-up, or feinted too fast, I felt like I was going to vomit. I knew it was time to stop fighting.

Months passed, and one Friday night, after I'd been out drinking in the Old Port, I came home to my empty apartment with a strange kind of hunger that I hadn't felt since I'd been in the ring. I knew there was no way to satiate the feeling. There was nothing like fighting and nothing that could fill the emptiness of not doing it. I am not sure what part of my brain told me to do this, but I wandered to the back of my apartment and turned on my computer. I searched

Jaed Coffin

online for record of "Mike Edenshaw, Juneau, Alaska." There was only one record: an obituary in the *Juneau Empire*.

The obituary said that about a year ago, The Nice Guy died of brain cancer. Survived by a wife and sons and daughters and grandchildren and great-grandchildren, the obituary also read that Mike Edenshaw, though he was known as The Nice Guy to boxing fans, was known as "Haida Mike" to friends and family. His favorite activities besides boxing were hunting, fishing, and carving. Many of his carvings could be seen in and around the cruise ship hotels along the Juneau waterfront.

What the obituary didn't say is that the Edenshaw name held some weight in the native cultures of Southeast. Charles Edenshaw, a deceased Haida carver whose work had pioneered a market among white collectors and who had helped the anthropologist Franz Boas to cultivate original studies on "primitive art," was a real source of dignity among his people. Charles' ancestor, Albert, was known as one of the great chiefs in the history of the Haida nation. Albert Edenshaw had probably been among that slim generation of Northwest Indians who'd known the land both before the arrival of the Russian and European fur traders and also after that time—when it had been farmed and Christianized, over hunted and over fished, and sold away. The night that I fought him, I knew nothing about this lineage and I did not know that the meaning of the Edenshaw name—derived from the old Tlingit word *Eda'nsa*—was used to describe things that were "melting away, like the ice of a glacier, until there is nothing left of it."

On the night that I fought him, I also did not know that three years later, in the same barroom, in the same ring, on the same canvas, Bob Haag would hold a Roughhouse benefit night to raise money for The Nice Guy's hospital bills. Though The Nice Guy wasn't well enough to attend, Haag had even presented members of the Edenshaw family with a plaque that read: "To a great boxer, Mike Edenshaw, from all your friends at Marlintini's."

I stayed up a while longer that night, wondering how I was supposed to feel about the fact that a man I had once fought was now dead. The Nice Guy and I had known each other for about three minutes total, and yet I could still remember the weight of his slow heavy glove on my cheek, the bony feeling in my fist when it hit his head, the flash of his sneakers as they hung there, brand-new and sparkle-red, in the spot light over the ring.

Later, I found myself digging into a desk drawer for an old pack of cigarettes. Sitting on my front steps, staring into the cold November night, I lit one, took a few drags, and then held it away from me. For several seconds, I watched the cigarette shorten and the smoke curl, and then, fixed on the dazzling cherry, I watched it melt away until there was nothing left of it.

Lynn McGee

Cheers

It's February,
edible garbage frozen,
no berries on branches,
no senior tossing bread crumbs,
or tourist winging limbs of salty,
giant pretzels to wily squirrels
and the park's lone,
lumbering,
half-mad raccoon.
It's a hungry month,
in the 'teens for two weeks now,
icicles clinging to the subway's
blackened ceiling,
New Yorkers emerging above ground
in a phalanx of down jackets,
small people bloated to mythic proportions,
large people swelling to the stature of gods—
tired gods hauling shopping bags,
briefcases, backpacks, babies swaddled
snug as larvae, migration efficient
till someone in bulky mitts fumbles
a steaming bucket of chicken legs
which tumble free,
pigeons clotting to peck at meaty pins
rolling across icy asphalt,
yellow cab slowing for the red light
as they laconically disperse—
then the scene goes off-script,

Lynn McGee

pedestrians flinch, a pigeon hit, mid-
take off, by the cab's brutish grill,
the stunned bird flapping
as if underwater,
skimming parallel to the ground,
then somehow breaking the surface,
shooting upward,
while we cheer.

Lynn McGee

The Tasmanian Wolf, and You

Suspended mid-stride in a Plexiglas box compact as a kennel,
the world's last Tasmanian Wolf, lithe as a coyote,
pale as surrender, stared into a stairwell of the American Museum
of Natural History, and I stood, useless mourner,
before its reconstructed presence, jostled by patrons rushing
to more spectacular displays—blue whale hovering improbable
as a dirigible, grimacing totems, dioramas' pastel deserts rivaling
any Hollywood set, the Museum repeating its busy life,
the Tasmanian Wolf enduring just beyond
those sloping marble steps,
till one afternoon the Plexiglas box was gone,
and no information clerk, no sleep-walking guard
could direct me to its new station, one beige-uniformed man
finally recalling, with somber authority, 'Oh yeah, that thing.
We had to put it in storage'; extinction, then,
not the final insult, and only this remaining—
that the Tasmanian Wolf, stripes fanning down its sides,
jaws springing 120 degrees wide and snapping
on the furtive heat of chickens; the Tasmanian Wolf,
tight, marsupial pouch padding its belly,
able to rise up on hind legs like an Egyptian god—
head of a dog, body of a man—and scan the horizon;
the Tasmanian Wolf is absent from its eucalyptus-tangled island,
from the concrete of zoos and stairwells of museums,
absent from the atmosphere and oxygen where it swirled into shape
over millions of years; absent, even, from memory, though I can see
those glass eyes gleaming in the dark of a storage closet,
and the frosty walls of that Plexiglas box holding everything

that's forever lost, no magic able to undo that silence,
animate that synthetic gaze,
and no harm in mourning the irretrievable—
love discarded, hope erased, kindness withheld,
talent let slip unnoticed as a scarf on the icy
sidewalk. Measure the immeasurable
damage your life's amassed, but leave your loss
in dark storage, and find something worth saving.

Allison Alsup

Stray

DOWN ON THE BEACH, THE MEN make their way towards the sampan. We watch as they step barefoot over the sand, one behind the other, slippers and boots tucked under their arms. On their shoulders, they carry bundled sheets with all their belongings. They have pinned up their braids beneath straw hats to keep their hair from snapping in the wind and their brown faces from the water's glare. A tobacco-colored dog follows the last man's heels. The four men have shared a cabin and the dog, a stray bitch that found its way into camp, has slept on their porch since the start of the season. It runs into the whispering waves. I have heard them call to this dog: Ma-cheuk. Sparrow. I have seen the last man feed this dog from his own rice bowl.

The dog bites at the water. It knows the boats. Since

the start of the season, it has ridden out with the men over dark waters and low tides. It has watched them anchor and stake the nets into the grassy bottoms at Black Point. It has shared the narrow benches as the men drank tea and smoked and sat until the sun came up. It has waited with them as the tide swelled, watched them pull the poles and empty the shrimp into the hull and sail back to camp. It has stayed with them in the sheds as they sorted and boiled the catch, laid the shrimp out to dry on the cleared hillside, winnowed the shells and sacked the dried meat. It has seen the men follow the tides, morning and evening, day in, day out, lowering and lifting the hemp nets sent across the ocean from Canton.

But here is what the dog does not know: American men cannot stand to see Chinese make money on Gold Mountain. It does not know that the Americans have passed a law shortening the season, ending it just when grass shrimp are their sweetest. It does not know that starting tomorrow, ghost patrols will sweep the bays for Chinese nets and men to send back to Canton. Nor does the dog know that these are SiYi County men, taught to fish by their fathers and grandfathers and their fathers and grandfathers before them, Delta men from the four counties. It does not know that these men, like all water men, cannot be made to stay in one place. It does not know these men light incense and pray to Tien Hou, goddess to fishermen, immigrants and wanderers, heavenly mother to all of us who have no fixed place in this world. The dog does not know any of these things, so it waits, like any other day, to be lifted into the boat.

We pretend not to watch the men leave. The time for handshakes and well wishing is over. Instead, we pretend to be busy with other tasks, sweeping the steps, reading yesterday's newspaper. An empty water bucket waits at my feet, but I make no move to fill it. Like the two washerwomen who test a row of trousers drying on the line, the buckets and brooms are excuses for waking so early on a Sunday. Even Wing, a gambler and the laziest man in camp, has risen to see the men leave. Shirtless, he dangles an American cigarette over the rotted grey railing of his cabin. Otherwise the camp is still: the boats beached, the nets rolled, the boiling sheds quiet. The last of the shrimp dries silently on the hillside. It is Sunday, a day for mahjongg and letters, for news from home and gossip, a day to spend money on sing song girls, noodles and lottery tickets across the bay in San Francisco, a day to hatch new plans, a day for leaving.

It is only the old timers who stare openly from their bench in front of the grocery. They do not raise a hand to wave. Long time gone from Pearl River, they have seen a thousand good-byes. Still, the old men seem bothered. Perhaps watching the young men reminds them of when they first came to Gold Mountain, when their bodies could shoulder sixty pound sacks. Or perhaps the young men remind them of when the end of the season meant the beginning of another, another place, another chance. Always there was something. Now nothing.

Behind me, the porch announces Shen's step. He looks down on the beach, sees the waiting sampan and grunts. He sips from the tea I have left him. He does not like to rise early but even more, he does not like to appear lazy like Wing.

"They are going then," he says, his voice heavy with last night's whiskey. His taste for American liquor has grown constant.

I point towards the boat. "Dabo, the dog. It thinks it is going with them."

Shen frowns, but not at the dog. He looks into his cup. His hands are as thick as a soldier's. Perhaps his tea has gone cold "It is a stray, didi," he tells me. "It will find another place."

For a moment I think that if I were the last man I would take the dog with me. But of course he cannot. He is a working man.

We watch the men push the sharp bow over the beach towards the water's edge. Already the sun is leaching the smells of seaweed and shrimp from the sand. The first man hands his slippers and bundle to the next, rolls his pants and wades into the bay. He steadies the curved sides of the sampan as the others climb in.

Below the bow, I can make out the bright outline of eyes repainted just yesterday—an old timer trick meant to help the boat find its way through fog and dark, to keep its hull safe from greedy shoals. They will never say so, but they are afraid I think. After today, the men will no longer be able to turn to one another. They will no longer calm themselves with the sound of one another's breathing in the dark. One stays with men in cabins, bunkrooms, boarding houses for three months, six or a year. For a time, they are like brothers and uncles, shih-zu, clan. Then the season ends and they are gone, moved on, and their names are added to all the others from seasons before. Eventually the names are forgotten. What remains is something else: a man's village, his walk, his hands.

Here is what I will remember about the last man, the one who fed the stray. This man drew in the sand with sticks. Close in, you could not tell, but from here, where Shen and I stay on the hill, the shapes revealed themselves: a rabbit, a dragon, a phoenix, all formed with the grace of a scholar's brush. All washed away come morning. My father drew like this, fishes and trees, in the margins of his letters. He had been to school paid for with Gold Mountain money. He did not need to hire a sidewalk fortune teller to write his letters or to read them as my mother did. I still have these letters. They are all I have.

Shen taps his empty cup on the railing. I fetch the teapot. As I pour, Shen says he has forgotten where the men are headed. I remind him: the first to wash dishes in San Francisco, another to pick artichokes in Castroville, the last two to push irons in a cousin's laundry in third city, Stockton. Shen says nothing. There is nothing to say. They are common jobs for common men. I am not surprised that Shen has forgotten such work for it is not the kind of labor that the son of a wealthy Nanhai merchant will ever have to know. But I know laundry work—men labor there only when nothing else can be found. As for the rest, they are the kind of jobs my own father had, the kind of work Suning County men are used to.

One by one, the men drop their bundles into the hull. When these men write to their families, they will not tell exactly of their new work. They will send money, and once a year, a photograph, of themselves posed in a borrowed silk robe and sitting in front of a painted screen or if they are lucky, a tight American woolen suit of their own purchase with the jacket pulled aside to reveal a pocket watch. When these men write about Gold Mountain, they will not say that they must work like coolies or clean dirty clothes and dishes like mui tsai, servant girls. In their letters, they will be head waiters and foremen, part owners of a clothing store. And they will all be returning soon or sending for wives and sons. Soon. A lie brought them to Gold Mountain and it is this lie that they will send back over the ocean.

There is a song women sing in the Pearl Delta about Guam San husbands. My mother learned it as a child and would sing it when my father had been gone too long:

If you have a daughter, do not marry her to a Gold Mountain man.
Out of ten years, he will not be in the bed for one.
The spider will spin webs on top of the bedposts,
And dust will cover one side of the bed.

Of course, the men in the boat are not thinking about this song. They are thinking that they are moving on, that the next job will be better like a lucky lottery ticket, the winning number in a white pigeon game just waiting to be cashed. They are telling themselves that they were right to leave their fathers' villages for new adventures. It is what we all must tell ourselves, even those of us who have never seen our father's village.

"I am going to Dai Fou tomorrow," Shen says as if he has not already told me a hundred times of his trip to the city.

I can tell he is displeased to see others moving on before him. For a man like Shen, this fishing camp is a jail. He is no shrimper and stays only because the cabins are cheap and because he cannot stand the crowded stink of city bunkhouses. This camp is miles from San Francisco, but with his boat, he may come and go. As soon as his clothing shop and its apartments are built in San Francisco, he will be gone and his parents can find him a suitable bride to bring back on the boat. Merchants are allowed wives.

"I am going inside," Shen says and turns away from the watching the men.

In the coming week, more will be leaving camp. Some will stay on to fish bass or to work in the brick foundry over the hill. Of course, the old timers will stay. They will die here. It is what Shen fears most: to work all one's life and to end with nothing. But most will leave this camp and if the law against summer nets continues, then few will return next year. There will be no profit in shrimping and this camp will become like the ones in the Sierras, scrub silver and gold towns where years ago, men like my grandfather and father once dug. Places found, places lost. That is Gold Mountain.

Shen reappears in the doorway. "Soon, yes?"

It is his way of telling me I am late with breakfast.

I say I must fetch water. In truth, I do not need more, but I walk down the hill towards the well all the same. The empty buckets swing from either end of the pole across my shoulders. Like the rest of the camp, I must watch until the boat is gone.

Within minutes, the bundles have been wedged under the benches and the men are ready. It takes so little time to leave. They step, one by one, into the boat. The last man touches the dog on the head, then pushes the stern from the sand and climbs in. The men do not talk to one another. They do not turn back to wave. It is as if they are no longer together, no longer here. The oars dip and the boat begins to pull away. My hand rests on the well handle, but I do not pump it. We watch the sampan drift over the blue brown of the water's skin. The wind is quiet today; the men must pump the oars to reach the open water. From the sand, the dog watches the boat as well, then barks. It steps into the water and barks again.

The rest of us continue to keep watch, not because we are wondering what will happen to the men—they will be swallowed by Gold Mountain. We watch because there is not one among us who does not wish, in some part, to call out: Hold the oars! I am coming! and to wade into the rising tide. We watch because it is ourselves we see on the water.

Suddenly, the boat stops. There is shouting. One of the men points to the water. Then I see it: the dog coming after the boat, its brown head bobbing in the waves. The last man yells at the dog and points to the shore. But the dog does not turn around and continues to swim towards the sampan. The others drop their oars and begin shouting as well. The boat tilts in the confusion, steadies itself. Then the last man drops into the shallows; the water reaches to his chest. He halfway swims and pushes himself towards the dog, grabs it by the back of its neck and brings it to the beach.

We watch as the man who drew dragons in the sand yells and then hits the dog. He does not call it Sparrow. He calls it stupid, a cunt and a shit. The dog cries out. An old timer stands from his bench and yells back at the last man, tells him it is not right to beat a loyal dog. One of the washerwomen calls that that old man is right.

"Ai-yah, leave the dog alone!"

But the last man does not stop and hits the mutt a second time, a third time. The dog limps away on crouched legs, its tail low and lays flat in the sand. The last man tries to keep yelling, but he cannot. He coughs as he chokes on his words. He hits his chest to clear it and kicks up a spray of sand. One fist in the air, he yells that he has always hated this place, its rotted cabins, its stink of fish. He says this camp is nowhere, a stretch of sand, nothing. He says we can waste our time if we want, but he is never coming back. We watch in silence as he walks over the sand to the water. The other men have not brought the boat back and so the last man must wade through the breakers. The others shift to the other side of the sampan while the man heaves himself over the edge. The other men take up their oars, but the last man does not row with the others. He sits with his face in his hands, his back curled like a boiled shrimp.

The sampan reaches the point and disappears; the waves fill in the wake and within moments, there is no sign the men were ever here. I pump the well as the old timers begin to talk story in front of the grocery, waving their hands and telling of the seasons when a boat could net four hundred pounds of shrimp a day, and of all the men who returned home with gold in their pockets. Wing crushes a cigarette and slips inside his cabin, no doubt to go to sleep off last night's drink. The washerwomen pull a table into the shade and play mahjongg, betting with pennies left in pockets by forgetful customers. I slide the second bucket under the spout. We pretend not to hear the dog's whining, to see it crouched lamely in the sand. Shen's words come back: it is only a stray; it will find another place. But Shen knows nothing of dogs, I think as I watch the second bucket fill with water. Nor has he been on Gold Mountain long enough to understand this: the only places we keep are the ones we make.

I call out. At the sound of its name, the dog raises its head, stands and looks around. Shen will not want the dog at first. He will think it too much trouble. But Shen is a Nanhai man and can be made to see what is in his interest: a guard dog, a thing to spoil until he marries. Besides, it will not be Shen who will care for the stray. I bend my knees, position the pole across my shoulders, balance the buckets. Settling the water, I call again and watch the dog move towards me.

Rachael Lyon

The Story of Simultaneity

It starts like this: one man leans
on the edge of a sidewalk,
waits for a break in the traffic
a distance away that means 3 or 4
seconds. He starts to bend
his weight over its axis, across
the threshold of his hips
and at the same time the silver Nissan
hushes back his hair and shirttail
he is gone, crossed over.
When this man was born
he knew buoyancy, knew a way
of breathing. He saw no color,
ate nothing green or savory.
Then one day in his mouth a noise
came and grew, and he knew then
to holler at it: the first cold,
first dry, first unshakeable hunger.
Today he ate red curry
at the table next to mine. I watched
him ask if it was really spicy,
watched him wince. At home
in my bed, a younger man waits
for me. Or doesn't wait. Or sleeps.
The story of that man in bed
is the story of red curry, of the
yellow-orange trace it leaves behind
and under things. It's the story
of the man leaning into tailwind,
his head craned left and right
and left again. The Nissan
sailed into his spine, lifted

The Story of Simultaneity

and set him down under a tree
on the sidewalk. And the people
in Khing Thai press their cheeks
against the front window to hear
the rank vitality of their screams.
If I hold my palms against my ears
and close my eyes I can hear the rush
of things, feel the heat in my mouth,
my neck tightening with panic.
My admission to this world
is wholly patronizing, my laugh
aromatic, my thoughts small music:
on and off. *Today I am with you*
he seemed to say. *Soon though,
night will fall right in.* Go now.

Alyssa Barrett

The Habits of Phonies and Living Things *[Exhibits]*

GIRAFFA CAMELOPARDALIS: in replica, full-size and anatomically correct, surrounded by papier-mâché trees that suggest a warmer climate. I blur my eyes and watch for movement; I want to be fooled. The museum guide tells us that in the wild, giraffes rub their necks against each other in battle and to achieve orgasm—usually it's the males who do it with other males. I giggle helplessly because of the word "orgasm." Grace says she's disappointed in the females, who simply nurture their young. Why do we have to be the predictable ones? Why can't we do something more impulsive?

We come to the museum for the air conditioning. It's one of those community days where admission is free. It is the hottest summer on record, the summer before I start eleventh grade. I've been helping Grace pack up her apartment into boxes on the days I'm not working as a waitress. The tour we join because it is there and Grace says she's in the mood to take all we can get.

Don't worry, the guide says. There's more: when kept in captivity, the giraffes get confused and lick things they shouldn't. Isn't that something?

Grace points at the replica's legs where the seams are cracked and the stuffing is showing and says we should get our money back.

We didn't pay anything, I say. Remember?

Still, she says. She turns to the tour guide. So, what do they lick?

The tour guide nods and tells Grace it's a good question. Poles, mostly, or any sort of barriers that confine them.

Can you blame them? Grace asks me. I can tell she's thinking things I want to understand and don't. She's old enough, but she isn't like a mom at all and she has never had kids.

She tells me she'll buy us a six-pack of beer to share if I help her keep packing instead. I'm underage so of course I say yes. Grace says, The sooner we get out of here, Cole, the better.

Elephantidae (Elephas, Loxodonta). Video installation: my AP biology teacher drags in the giant monitor and fiddles with the controls until an image pops up and takes motion. It is an elephant holding a paintbrush in its trunk. The elephant faces an easel, draws with ink. This particular elephant has become famous for its ability to draw an elephant.

Everyone is fascinated: How can it know itself so clearly? My classmates and I are awkward and anxious. We are misunderstood. We write poetry on the covers of our notebooks and on the rubber soles of our sneakers. I imagine leaving home, traveling, being old enough to be sure of things. I write this in a postcard to Grace, who sends one back. We do this because she has moved two states away from where I live with my parents. She's started a new research job at one of the colleges where I've applied. I am still waiting to hear if I'll get in.

Grace says she gave an elephant a bath in India. She says she hiked the Himalayas, meditated, she learned what to do with tamarind and turmeric powder, kissed a monk, fell for a street vendor. *That part didn't last*, she writes. *But the rest was worth it. Here's another thing you won't like.* The elephants that draw, she tells me, are trained to move their trunks according to signals the keeper gives on the animal's ears. The keeper tugs left or right or up or down, and the elephant's trunk will follow. *Sorry. The elephants are awfully sweet to play along like that, though. If it were me, with that giant body, I'd opt for trampling.*

What I like is that she acts like I'm not seventeen and she's not forty-five. Like we're moving through a similar life, wondering similar things. I walk into one of those hippie stores downtown that sells incense and beads and try on a batik elephant-print dress that doesn't fit. My boobs don't fill the cups, which pouf out with extra material.

They make things for that, the store clerk says. She flips two rubber pads at me that look like chicken breasts. Put them in, hon, she says and laughs. Fake it till you make it.

I put the rubber pads against my skin, look at the unfamiliar shape of me in the mirror, the way the tiny elephants on the cloth march up and over the new curves.

Equus africanus asinus: often referred to as donkey, burro, ass. This one I read about in the newspaper and I put it in the notebook I've started to keep. *Exhibits*, I call it. I fill the pages with animal facts I discover on TV and in books. When I can't fall asleep, I watch the animal and nature channels. I read through a set of encyclopedias I have found in the attic, and paste in articles and make notes.

The donkey described in the weekend newspaper article is painted with stripes using black hair dye blocked out with masking tape, to look like the zebras at the zoo where the one real zebra died. The real zebra was flown in during better days, but now it cannot be replaced. This is all happening on the other side of the world, where I have never traveled, in a country that surely has bigger but less fascinating problems than this.

The zookeepers there already tried smuggling tigers; it wasn't worth it. The article says the children are happy to see something new.

Meanwhile, here, in the land of real zebras, I read the news to Grace over the phone: how nothing goes in or out and yet the hair dye is plentiful. Grace says she wonders if they use her preferred shade. Her hair turned grey early and she doesn't like the look of it that way.

How are you? she asks, and I know she knows that I'm probably not doing so hot. In the last week, I was caught stealing eye shadow at the local drug store, nearly failed a math test and was told by the soccer coach that I was better suited for the junior varsity team again, even though everyone else in my grade made varsity. These are my own less fascinating problems.

I'm great, I say. Better than a zebra.

Camouflage, I later write on a new notebook page, *is a way to hide. It can be a handy tool in various situations. See also: blending in, lying, surviving.*

The Habits of Phonies and Living Things [Exhibits]

Otter subfamily *Lutrinae*; part of the family *Mustelidae*. An otter's den is called a *holt* or *couch*. A male otter is a *dog*, a female a *bitch*, and a baby a *whelp* or *pup*. Otters are often playful in nature. The collective nouns are *bevy*, *family*, *lodge* or *romp*, or when in water, *raft*. I called Grace *aunt* until I was fourteen. I thought that's what she was. When my parents went out, she babysat and we built forts out of the couch cushions and ate whipped cream colored with food dye. My mom said I'd misunderstood: Grace used to date my uncle Joe, but it didn't work out. Don't you remember? she said. We stayed friends, but it's better not to bring it up. It was kind of complicated in the end.

Grace came to dinner at our house every week when she still lived in town. She was beautiful, always in bright lipstick. You can still call her *aunt*, my mom said.

Rattlesnakes, genera *Crotalus* and *Sistrurus*, belonging to the subfamily of venomous snakes known as *Crotalinae* (pit vipers). I have never had a boyfriend. I've kissed but only during truth-or-dare, which, no matter who you ask, doesn't count. During Bio, I watch the way my childhood best friend, Victor, dissects a worm. We have been assigned as lab partners, which makes it easier because we can both pretend we don't care. He has stubble on his face. I can't place when he started to look like this. Victor takes some worm guts in his fingers and smashes them and holds the goo close to my face. If we kissed, it might be messy. I stay up late to think about it. Instead of doing homework, I watch the nature channel and I see something that looks like a worm for a flash: it's a documentary on rattlesnakes. They grow a new rattle each time they shed their skin. When the rattles get too wet, they soak up water and make no noise when they move. I watch until I fall asleep and I have a dream that I later ask Grace—who has always been good with dreams—to interpret. But she won't do it; she says this one is for me to figure. In the dream, snakes crawl underneath the door to my room and up the edges of my bed. They surround me and start rattling like crazy, a deafening whoosh. I don't want to chop off their heads. I don't wonder if they'll strike. I just listen to the noise of them and wish that someone else were there to witness it. Even in the dream, I know there are no words for such a sound. I say, *Shhh*, to the snakes and they listen and we wait.

Danaus plexippus (subfamily *Danainae*), in the family *Nymphalidae*. When Monarch butterflies migrate, not one butterfly that started the trip makes it back. Instead, it might be a fourth-generation butterfly baby that ends up doing the final leg. It seems a crazy, instinctual impulse, for that first butterfly to want to head south if it will never know north again. Maybe it thinks it will last, maybe it thinks it wants a vacation; maybe it doesn't think at all.

Grace doesn't date anyone for years after Uncle Joe. Sometimes, she wants to talk about him. She tells me he has a fascinating brain. How many men do you meet where you're just really boggled by their mind? she asks. I was always trying to figure him out, she says. I didn't fascinate *him* enough. Go figure.

To me, it is impossible. Grace, with her lipstick and dark hair and complicated research job, her apartment decorated with exotic rugs and the way she laughs and makes everyone feel like they're stronger than they are. If she isn't enough, I can't imagine where I'm headed.

I blame Uncle Joe for everything, for not being fascinated, for giving up. It's probably more complicated, I know, but I'm fiercely loyal to Grace. If I could make a blood relative trade, him for her, I'd do it. Uncle Joe travels for work and rarely makes it to family events, anyway. When he does, I am cold toward him. He asks me about school and I answer in a word. He wants the plate of broccoli passed to him at Thanksgiving, and I make him ask twice. I think mean things, like how he's balding and boring and probably will die alone. I am eighteen and righteous and after dinner I call Grace at her sister's house, where she is spending the holiday with her real family. She tells me about her nephews and her relatives, none of whom I've met. I have the fleeting thought that I've been wrong all along: I assumed she thought I was her family, too. I can't think of what to say after a while. Grace has told me before she hates small talk and thinks its better to be weird than boring, so I ask her what she's wearing. I want to hear her tone shift, I want her to fall into the odd language we have together. And it works: she laughs through the phone.

Good one, Cole, she says. I'm wearing a space-suit negligee and have an accordion around my neck so I can entertain the humanoids. Would you like to hear my beautiful song?

Ondatra zibethicus. The muskrat's name comes from the two scent glands found near its tail—they give off a strong "musky" odor, which it uses to mark its territory. It is early fall when I go to visit Grace in her new house. I've been accepted at a different college, not in the same town where Grace lives, but

The Habits of Phonies and Living Things [Exhibits]

not too far away, either. I have a crappy car I bought with money saved up from another summer waitressing job, and I drive the forty-five minutes out to see her.

She says she likes the open space and the easy parking. The ocean is only twenty minutes away, and we make plans to go in the summer. In the meantime, we break a bottle of sparkling cider over the railing while her new neighbor scowls.

I can hear you pee, the neighbor says. You keep the window open like that and I can hear it. Why don't you close your goddamn window so I don't have to hear you do your dirty business?

Because it's *my* business, says Grace. I like it breezy.

Grace convinces me to stay the night. It's not hard. I'm so far confused by college, which is better than high school but still crowded with girls who bond and giggle over frozen yogurt. The friends I've made are the people who bum cigarettes outside the dorm, who stay late in the science lab on weekend nights like I do. It's reassuring and yet nothing to miss, either.

We decide we'll build a fence in her backyard, where herbs and vines can grow high enough that Grace can pretend no one else is there.

So much for the suburbs, she says.

I offer to plant poison ivy in the neighbor's yard. Grace says maybe she'll get a dog instead, a German Shepherd or Rottweiler—something protective and territorial.

Maybe something that doesn't *pee*, I say.

Vietnamese: *Lon in:* shown as a domesticated pet, as seen on the dorm's basement TV. In instances of misbehavior: Say "NO" in a firm, strong voice. Push the pig by the shoulders to the side and divert him from his intent. This is how two pot-bellied pigs normally fight. They push each other around from the side at the shoulders. Try clapping your hands. You are communicating that this is not allowed behavior. Try changing your tone. Try singing to the pig: *Little piggy goes to market, ei-yi-ei-yi-oh.* Try crafting a sculpture from capillary tubes melted in a Bunsen burner, a cork and a rubber hose. Try ignoring the messages from home. Try sleeping, burrowed in blankets in a shared living space. Try getting laid—try, try, and feel embarrassed for trying too hard when what you were going for was a feeling of empowerment, independence. Try leaving the lab behind: maybe there's more to it than just biology.

Try calming the pig with a bowl of warm milk. Try returning the pig to the shelter where you found it. Say, this was never meant to be a pet.

Bees, of the superfamily *Apoidea*. In danger but not endangered; subject to colony collapse disorder. After making it through my second year of college, now as an English major, I fall in love with a beekeeper. He says he orders his bees by Express mail—that they arrive in a box with his name on it, that they don't buzz at all; in fact it is eerie-silent and the box weighs almost nothing when it comes. He takes me out to the hive he's built in his backyard; he gives me gloves and a hat with netting.

He says he doesn't need protection, that the secret to not getting stung is to become one with the bees. To think kind thoughts toward them.

I think I am doing it, but he comes away clean and my skin swells and burns from being stung, and I am choking for air. He has to jab me with an epinephrine pen. I think of Grace, who told me she nearly choked on a noodle from her soup. She had to give herself the Heimlich against a chair, because there was no one else there to save her.

Crickets. Note: have previously failed to notice the chirping insects' inhospitable behavior, which is a lesson that might've been learned already. When trapped from the campus herb garden and left alone in a fish tank with a plate on top in a dorm room, they will not eat leftovers. Rather, they will eat each other, and they'll do it as quickly as possible. One dominant, bloated cricket will remain. He will then die of his own gluttony, because his small body cannot digest the other cricket parts fast enough.

Popillia japonica, commonly known as the Japanese beetle: iridescent copper-colored wings, and green thorax and head. In Japan, it has predators, but here it feeds on the same things we do, unbothered and therefore highly threatening to our vegetation: strawberries and tomatoes and roses and hops.

Grace has never liked beer and always keeps flowers on her table, even in winter. The Japanese beetle also eats blackberries, cherries, grapes and blueberries. I haven't seen Grace in over a year—I've moved in with the beekeeper, who now keeps the bees away from me. He and I live in a new town where I have an assistant job. It takes five hours, this time, to drive to Grace's house, which smells the same as ever: herby and warm. We buy blueberry wine instead of regular because we are curious. It tastes like old juice, but I sort of like the strange flavor of it. She tells me about the dates she's been on, the men who fail to interest her for more than a few evenings. She winds up talking again about Uncle Joe, how she knew they weren't meant to be, how she was too young, how they both liked to cook and read the same books, how she thought that he was different from the monk or the banker or the artist or any of the others. I feel lucky about the beekeeper and say as much, then wonder if I have found something that Grace hasn't. I wonder if she is jealous. I wonder if I finally know something she doesn't.

We finish two bottles. I am dizzy and realize that it was mostly me drinking and Grace has barely finished a second glass. She steps out of the room frequently. She says she feels fine, perfect, better than that. She says I should come back in the spring or the summer. She says, That beekeeper is a *keeper*, Cole. She laughs her great laugh, which doesn't sound as great as usual. She says, We've got nothing but time.

I sense she's indulging me when she says of course I must stay the night. I'm too drunk to argue. I lay across her couch like it's my own, I call the beekeeper just to hear him say he loves me. The Japanese beetle is a clumsy flier and when it hits a wall, it falls several centimeters before it realizes what's happened.

Strigidae, genus Megascops: primarily solitary, but during the late-winter breeding season, male screech owls make nests in cavities, sometimes reusing abandoned nests of other animals. The females select their mate based on the quality of the cavity and the food located inside. Grace is fifty-three and single and I am twenty-five and brokenhearted. It hasn't taken all that long for me to bore the beekeeper into finding someone else, and he has left me with an empty hive behind our apartment; he has taken the bees. Grace and I imagine starting a commune together. She'll leave her research work and I'll abandon my job, which still involves spending all day in a cubicle. We make a list of the people we'll invite to visit and another list of the people we won't. We'll keep sheep and make cheese and grow all our own vegetables. Grace will learn to can and pickle things for the winters, and she tells me I can take up knitting and pottery. I am surprised, suddenly, by how far we've taken it, by how emphatic Grace is about this dreamy plan. Even in the newness of the beekeeper's absence, I know we'd never actually *do* it. But she uses a certain voice, like she really believes it could happen. I play along. She says we'll teach ourselves how to play the banjo. We'll fix our own fences. I say it sounds brilliant, that I can't wait. It'll be so great, I say.

But I've gone too far. Grace makes a face. You know, she says, you don't have to end up like me. You can do way better.

Of the *Accipitridae* family, as seen on the presidential seal and on the backs of old quarters. Grace encountered one, many years ago, before they stopped showing up as often. She climbed a mountain alone, stripped down at the top just because she could, watched the sky for hours. She said once the eagle saw her, he circled her over and over again, as if it was a sign of something.

Canis lupus, often known simply as *wolf*. Hunts in packs; attacks till its prey is just flesh and bones and blood in the snow. Grace never gets a German Shepherd, but she does get a tattoo. She sends a photo. It's abstract and outdoorsy, something like a wolf among trees, a howl in blues and greens. It's on her upper arm, on the thin, inside skin. She says it bled and bruised at first, but now it feels great. You should try it, she says. What would you get?

I can't answer. I don't know what would mean enough. An equation? I say. Where I'm living now, alone and in a spacious new apartment, is in a small, rural town, where I've decided I might find some sort of a life that more closely resembles how I thought things would be. I have finally followed Grace's advice: my latest job is teaching earth science at the local school. I spend the days in a classroom lab again, this time cleaning the equipment, correcting lab reports and leading experiments. At home, I bake loaf after loaf of bread because I like the kneading. After eating nothing but bread for what seems like weeks, I get a craving for meat. It comes on strong. I'm hiking alone in the woods on a weekend afternoon. I absurdly consider the odds that I'll come across a cow on my path; wonder if I'd have what it takes to wrestle it to the ground. And then what—tear up its flesh with my hands? Eat its bloody muscles with my fingers? It occurs to me that maybe what I want and need is a man. Something real. I think of the few local guys I have tried dating, of teenage Victor and the beekeeper, both of whom I no longer know. Nothing sticks. What I can get is a steak, and at the supermarket I have the butcher cut thick, heavy strips of beef. I am impatient as it cooks. The first bite satisfies; I eat the rest too quickly and feel sick. I still haven't figured out how to want something properly.

Caterpillars of *Geometridae* [frequently: inchworm], less than 2.5 cm in length. I watch it crawl across a beam on my back porch in the rain, until he

The Habits of Phonies and Living Things [Exhibits]

belly-flops into a puddle, plays dead in a pool of water. I find out from my mother that they have given Grace a bad diagnosis and I can barely get her on the phone. I leave messages and finally she sends a note back in response. She tells me she was going to call, but she's trying not to dwell on it. She's spending time with her sisters and nephews. She's had tests but they don't know exactly how bad it is yet. She'd like me to visit, but maybe we can schedule something later. She's doing yoga, she's trying to be Zen. I wait for her to say something weird and funny, like she's also trying to practice the Hustle on a daily basis, but she doesn't.

I swear at the inchworm. I can't stand the not knowing. Like a child, I tell the inchworm I want him to live. I tell him he is an asshole and a traitor and would it kill him to pick up the damn phone? I put him on a napkin to help him dry out, and I move the corners up and down, some small measure of resuscitation. I watch for his movements and start to cry when I see his body arch up again in life, searching for solid ground. I place the inchworm, still on the napkin, on a part of the porch that's dry and protected by an eave. Later, I come back and the napkin is empty.

Turdus migratorius, commonly known as a *robin*, which is trying to make a nest in the rafters above my front door. It collects sticks and strands of blue tarp from the neighbor's yard; it tries and fails to make a whole nest. The half-nests keep dropping to the ground. Perhaps out of frustration or some sort of bird disease, the robin smears its feces against my kitchen window. It dries in white, wing-patterned arcs that are almost pretty. I can hear the bird thump against the glass. Eventually, there is a full nest up in the rafters. The bird comes and goes and no longer messes up the window. I assume there is an egg but I don't check. I want the bird to feel at home.

In the classroom, I show my students how to use test tubes and litmus paper. I demonstrate how the incubator works, how to handle a fertilized egg. I tell them there are no guarantees. The kids look like this is the most important thing they have ever done—this, which in their brains rivals the space for remembering locker combinations, equations, vocabulary words, pacts and secrets between friends. Together, we place the eggs inside the incubator and hope that they will come alive.

Note: Grace doesn't want chemo or radiation. The kind she has turns out to be the kind that's everywhere before you even feel it. I'd rather be myself till—whatever, she says. Not some hairless, puking thing. She finds a healer who gives her paintbrushes and tells her to draw the disease out from under her skin with art. Grace laughs at this part. I want my money back, she says.

Macrochelys temminckii, from the lake outside of town, which appears in the rumors from swimming children. I have yet to catch sight of it. I only see it in sleep, in dreams that I can't interpret. I imagine that Grace would say it is obvious. She would tell me: You are you and I am the fingers and the snapping turtle won't let go. Don't you see? But all I know is this: The pain is sharp and the water becomes bloody, and my hand doesn't look like my own.

Struthio camelus, large and flightless, with a long neck and legs and the ability to run at maximum speeds of about 70 km/h (45 mph). They say ostriches can run faster than any bird in the world. When threatened, an ostrich might run away, because it is faster than most of its predators. It is always her sister that calls me now. On the good days, Grace's sister tells me they go for walks in the sun because Grace is still herself. On the not-so-good days, they make ginger tea and Grace lies under blankets. The sister tells me, I'll be in touch, but she isn't and after a while I'm afraid to call because who am I, anyway? I busy myself with correcting student papers and scheduling unnecessary meetings with fellow teachers just for the company. When an ostrich senses a threat it can't outrun, it will hide itself by lying flat against the ground, so it looks like a mound of earth.

Menura novaehollandiae: a mocking, mimicking bird which can sound like a chainsaw because workers showed up in the rainforest with chainsaws and orders to follow. The bird can make the sound of a tree coming down with its throat, like it knows what it is saying.

The Habits of Phonies and Living Things *[Exhibits]*

Pinniped (from Latin *pinna*, wing or fin, and *ped-*, foot): *Otariidae* (external ears). Finally Grace tells me to come. She leaves it in a message and we don't actually speak until we're face-to-face. Even then, we're mostly quiet. I drive us to the beach near her house even though it's not summer. It is early spring and too cold, still, to be busy. Ours is the only car in the lot. We walk down the boardwalk, over sand dunes and tall grasses, to the shore. The sun is bright. She is thin. I resist the urge to take photos because I don't like what it means. Grace's hair, thinner but still dark, moves in the wind. She says she can feel the heat inside her, moving, even though her skin is cold beneath her layers of sweaters. We stand at the ocean's edge, shivering. I'll do it if you do, she says. I know I should discourage her, I should be responsible and remind her this isn't safe, it isn't practical, it could cost her. But I am starting to understand that I don't understand anything, and I still believe, so deeply, that she does. We leave our clothes in a pile on the sand and run into the water. Our legs go numb almost immediately, and I help her limp back to shore and we sit in the sun. I don't take another photograph. Look, Grace says and I do. Out in the water, a seal makes its way, rising and disappearing below the surface.

Jodie Marion

nichos

a boy scatters
pigeons or maybe
light. hard to tell.

a woman prays.
god sits inside the
box & plays along.

a blue heron plucks
koi from a pond, gets
a standing ovation.

a dentists traps
a woman, drills
and proselytizes.

epiphany in car-
wash: product
of circumstance.

a girl jumps
off a wax boat,
sprouts wings.

a woman dies,
a still bird in
a soft white nest.

a jar of fish bones
sucked clean.
no one in sight.

a family swallows
something more
invention than food.

a church marquis
reads: verse, joke,
potluck & apocalypse.

an angry boy lobs
a black cloud at
his brother's heart.

the tide washes
away an anthol-
ogy of regret.

two people in bed:
two coastlines
around a gulf.

the greatest act
of indecency: he
ignores beauty.

night after night,
we people our
unholy nation.

Penelope Scambly Schott

His Eye

Somewhere where terrible things happen—
not here, though terrible things do happen—
but somewhere they happen more frequently
(and I read about this, I didn't see it first hand),
a boy was beaten so fiercely that one eyeball
fell out of his head, and he carried his own eye
safe in the palm of his hand over many miles
to the nearest doctor and begged the doctor
please to sew his eye back in its raw socket
but of course the doctor couldn't sew it back
(I suppose the optic nerve was severed and
who knows what all else) so that loose eye
was thrown out or buried, who knows which,
because that detail wasn't in the story I read,
but here's what I do know: forever afterward
the boy's hand, the hand that carried the eye,
was gifted with vision. If he touched a stone,
he knew the hidden inside color of that stone,
and when he grew up and touched a woman,
he knew, more fully than anyone else could,
all the untold dread that made her beautiful.

Marcia Popp
the music lesson–december 1943

one night when it was not my father's turn to help with the air raid drill he carried me outside during the blackout wrapped against the cold inside his warden's greatcoat under a night sky not dimmed by city lights…as we listened to the sirens sing a shrill b-flat minor up and down the streets my father told me it was the dark key like rachmaninoff's piano sonata and the oboe solo in tchaikovsky's 4th symphony…over the wail of sirens the stars arranged themselves as glittering notes on the staff of the tall oak branches spread high above us my father said the stars were closer that night than he had seen them since he was a boy…as we watched them brilliant back the darkness their sparkling drowned out the sounds of sirens and we stayed there until the drill was over listening to them shine.

Eileen Annie

Saturday's Child Remembered

>*Something is going*, I said,
>causing a nod barely parting the air
>as if it was heard, as if it was said.

I met with someone today and had ice cream and no tea
at that sunny deli in the shopping mall with the seaside
motif. We talked about saving the world and the children
or she talked and I listened
as I couldn't think to answer before the words gushed out,
not the right words, not the words I thought to say
until I got past that and there was passion
equal to her eyes and coral gauze sundress
glimmering in window refractions—
passion for saving the children and then the world
in that order.

>*Something is going, it sits heavy*
>*in the bones and joints like dampness*
>*and cold rooms, this sense of going*
>*unspoken as a silenced tea pot, motionless*
>*as the gathering of sea gulls in a sunny deli.*

I called the boys yesterday mid-day.
They supposed it odd me calling mid-day
and I odd they were together on a Saturday
when they don't see each other
when they don't work
in that order,
and still the words were gushing and jumbled,
myriads of short choppy utterances in need of translation,

Eileen Annie

not at once the words I thought to say
until I got past that and they could not see
I thought it was Saturday.

> *Something is going, as yesterday, as Saturday*
> *as a nod barely parting the air, going in a sense*
> *unspoken and motionless and unseen,*
> *going as things not wanted*
> *and lives changed,*
> *and gripped emotions slipping inside like snakes*
> *from a lifetime of words.*

And I want to say it is everything
and everything is like that—not wanting
and passionate and short and gripping and finally
in translation with no comprehendible answer, only

> *something is going*

Something is going,
where the ping in darkness is unreachable
where the sound is tired, and raw, and clinging by chance
for existence on its own wanton wings—
and what is left, and visible, and disordered, are pieces
of shattered stained glass prisms in the sun's light
and words not understood.

Excerpted from The Last of the Khazars, *a novel in progress*

Judith Podell

The Muse

> *She gets effects which a trained singer would try in vain to achieve among us and which are only produced precisely because her means are so inadequate.*
> —Franz Kafka, Josephine the Singer, or the Mouse Folk

I WAS MURDERED BY A NAZI in 1930, in the alley behind the White Mouse Cabaret, which is where I got my start. Music critics used to describe my voice as "partially ravaged" and "the howl of an aging cat in heat." I had a strong following among homosexual men and brokenhearted women, but I also attracted attention from the ones in uniform, always standing in the back to make it look like they were on business. We called them the Gerhardts, after one of the nasty little songs I used to sing. This particular one waited in the shadows the way he'd seen Kurt do. Whispered my name. I knew it wasn't Kurt but turned around anyway. Silver blond hair cut short, like bristles. Big pink rigid face. Small gray eyes. Too clean.

He was a brown shirt with friends on the police force so he knew he could get away with murder. Kurt was charged with the crime, then shot in the head "while resisting arrest." My family was secretly relieved. I was their shame, a disgrace to the Katzenbachs with their big dark apartment in the best available neighborhood and so eager to believe the police cared about bringing to justice the killer of a Jew. My death was a piece of luck for the authorities. It was Kurt they were after, not me. He wrote for leftist journals, a dangerous occupation.

We are dead men on furlough, he used to remind me.

We used to say that to cheer each other up those last nights in Berlin, watching the world end. No time for secrets or standing on ceremony.

And I would sing for him our private songs:

> *behind the dirty houses by the factory*
> *our stars have turned to broken glass*
> *we meet in Hell's waiting room*
> *& smoke leftover cigarettes*

Up on stage that night I wore black stockings and a tuxedo jacket, that hint of drag, boy on top and girl on bottom. A touch of perversity, my little riding crop and a Charlie Chaplin Hitler mustache. Heavy red lipstick. Like one of those trick drawings that are two things at once. Is it der Fuhrer or is it a smiling vagina? I sat on a chair backwards flaunting my fine legs and sang my nasty songs that drove the Gerhardts crazy.

> *Hans is deaf and Franz is lame*
> *And Heinz can hardly see.*
> *Gerhard has a tiny dick*
> *He likes to watch me pee.*
> *The crippled men all want me as their girlfriend*
> *One touch of Venus in their price range.*

The one in the back who kept trying to catch my eye, he'd been in before. Silver bristle hair, piggy face. Sometimes I made eye contact with the Gerhardts long enough to cause them embarrassment.

The Muse

"You know what they say: Once a philosopher, twice a pervert," I called out to Silver Bristles. "Why not come up front and enjoy the show."

I'd taken him for one of the harmless ones, half-hoped he'd take me up on the challenge so I could incorporate him into the act and was mildly disappointed when he turned and left. All my instincts were off that night. A stupid fight with Kurt made me reckless. Of course he had a girl on the side, but when did he not?

We used to play that we were strangers; no words, just quick anonymous sex in the alley. The sound of footsteps on cobblestones one cool, rainy night, and I was in heat like the little cats we used to mock.

The footsteps didn't sound right, that night. Too heavy, but I wanted it so to be Kurt.

The Afterlife has all the discomforts of home: Sunday dinners of overcooked beef and boiled potato, glass-fronted cabinets displaying Dresden china and porcelain figurines. Respectable people carry on the same inane conversations, word for bloody word. Over high tea at the Metropole, Madame Weil and Frau Wittgenstein promote the kind of match that could only be made in Purgatory.

With eternal life you get eternal hope, usually in vain.

"They have much in common," Frau Wittgenstein tells Madame Weil. "Your daughter is a philosophy student while my son is a philosopher."

Madame Weil is too conventional to point out to Frau Wittgenstein that her daughter Simone is also a full-fledged philosopher. She would have preferred grandchildren.

Kafka is nowhere in sight. Perhaps the Admissions Committee is biased towards writers. Meanwhile all his girlfriends and pen pals congregate at the Café Vienna. Each of us knew a different Franz. Felice Buaer's Franz was her fiancé, Herr Doctor Kafka of the Prague Workman's Compensation Board, an authority on industrial safety who wrote odd little stories for a hobby.

Mine loved the Yiddish actors and courted women he had no intention of marrying, like my cousin, Felice.

Dora's Franz, the last, was a Zionist saint who wrote little fables, most of which she destroyed, the fool.

He was my first love. Meeting him set me in motion.

Who can explain the desire to express oneself in the absence of encouragement or visible talent? I just knew there was something first-rate and extraordinary in me that demanded its existence be known to strangers.

I was different from the others: dark haired, a big mouth, and too much activity in my face. "More Jewish-looking," Mama used to say, as though this was something shameful. Yet they professed to be proud of being Jews, proud to resist the pull of conversion even as they praised my younger sister for her little nose and light hair as though she had cleverly picked the genetic traits from some remote Viking ancestor.

"That one will be hard to marry off," Mama said once, thinking I was out of earshot.

Papa said he'd be proud of me if I grew up to be a businesswoman like our cousin Felice Bauer, who held a responsible position with a Berlin firm that manufactured office equipment; nonetheless, a woman's true vocation was wife-and-motherhood.

Poor Felice, with those terrible teeth, all big and so crowded in her mouth, like a boisterous family in a two-room apartment.

Hard for me to decide which future held less charm: wife-and-motherhood or the office. Always having to sit still. Always someone standing over you, looking to find fault.

Men always say they don't want children, but that just means they don't like other people's children, according to Felice. She is sure her fiancé will feel differently about children after he marries her. He is so intelligent, but in many ways young for his years, still like a schoolboy with his passionate friendships. Why, he still lives with his family, and the father can be loud and overbearing. The mother seems lovely, wanting only her son's happiness, but Papa rules. Married life will be different for dear Franz. He'll be the man of the house. And possibly he won't want to write nearly as much. Especially after the children come. You can't make a living from writing strange little stories that no one reads.

The night they first met, at Max's Brod's house, she introduced herself to his friend, Dr. Franz Kafka, and they shook hands, very businesslike. Max was distant family and something of a matchmaker. At dinner Felice and dear Franz sat across from each other. Promise me you'll come with me to Palestine next year, he said. Very well, she'd said, and thought it an idle remark, not to be taken seriously. A bold bit of small talk.

Five weeks later she received the most charming letter from him suggesting they begin to plan their upcoming holiday. And more letters, letters demanding detailed response. He wants to know everything about her. The view from her window. What she is reading? What she ate for breakfast and does she take sugar with her coffee? He wants to know of her friends at the office and their daily habits. He is fascinated by the minutiae of his own life as well. If someone told you every little thing he did in the past hour, leaving nothing out including the sugar in the coffee, wouldn't you flee? But it was different, coming from him.

What a face he had. Like a fox or faun. Pointed ears would not have been out of place.

You felt the full force of his personality in his gaze, an impersonal intimacy he extended to each of us at the engagement party, where he was introduced to everyone related to Felice by blood or marriage. So much family there was not enough air to go around. The men all bluff and stuffing, and the women full of pride and anxiety. His manner grave and courtly, as though he was an ambassador from a small country and I was a personage of equal importance instead of a school girl in a dress with too many ruffles.

"Miss Hannah," he said, and for one giddy moment I thought he might ask me to join him in Zion, "Promise me that you will make every effort to see the Yiddish theater troop when they come to Berlin," he said. He loved their irreverence and vitality; thought I might be the sort of person who appreciated these characteristics.

"But I don't understand a word of Yiddish."

The language of *Ostjuden*, Jews who come from backwards Poland. Jews who embarrassed us, cast doubt upon our hard-won refinement.

"Of course you understand Yiddish, Miss Hannah," he said. "You just don't realize it. Yiddish is the mother of all languages; in fact it was German that broke off from Yiddish, not the other way around."

"Don't let Felice hear you say that," I said.

Anyone could see there was no heat between the two of them. They didn't belong together in the same room.

Judith Podell

June, 1914

Esteemed Dr. Kafka:

You will probably not remember me. We met very briefly last May in Berlin when you visited the family of Felice Bauer, who is my father's cousin. We spoke about the Yiddish actors and I promised you I would seek them out when they come to Berlin. It is never too soon to prepare for such a great venture. Would you be so kind as to advise me which actors are the finest or recommend a course of study?

Sincerely,
Hannah Katzenbach

Seducing my cousin's fiancé is wrong and dangerous but the temptation is irresistible, and I can't stop—anymore than I can stop masturbating whenever I have the chance to be alone, which isn't often. I imagine our bodies igniting, a dance of nerves and muscle, all his intensity driven into me, the darkness but also fire.

8 June 1914

My Dear Fraulein Katzenbach:

Among what appeared to be a sea of mounted resignation, yours was the only welcoming face. As to your request for guidance nothing can prepare you better than to look into your own heart and imagine how you might respond to the world without the questionable benefit of formal education and freed from the obligation to be useful or dignified. Now you must tell me how your day begins. A typical day, please. What do you study in school? What do you read for pleasure?

With kindest regard,
Franz K.

The Muse

14 June 1914

Dear Herr Doctor Kafka,

In answer to your questions: I eat soft-boiled eggs for breakfast. In school I study the art of yawning with my mouth closed; the many irritating mannerisms of our teachers; and History, in which Germany is always triumphant because God is German. My favorite writer, besides you, is Dostoevsky.

Yours truly,
Hannah K.

I am not dear Franz's only correspondent, merely his most recent. All along he's been writing intimate confiding letters to Felice's so-called best friend Grete Bloch. Love letters, one might think. How he missed her presence at the engagement party which would have made the occasion bearable. He wished he could be holding her hand, rather than her letter.

The engagement is off.

Mama strikes a separate match for each letter he sent me, drawing out the little death.

"We will say nothing of this to your father," she says with a cold little smile.

I would prefer a beating to this unwanted intimacy. Her face too close to mine.

The next day I buy a one-way ticket to Prague.

The European erotic imagination owes much to the steam engine. Those little compartments with the doors and shades, not to mention the thrill of entering those tunnels. Like those dark places we all come from and cannot go home to. I have a compartment all to myself, such a pleasure. It will be easy to find dear Franz, because there are only two cafes in Prague where writers gather. All his friends, writers, journalists, and the one philosopher, are desperate to get out of Prague and move to Berlin or Vienna. All of them working up the courage to escape.

I find them at the Central, and introduce myself, hoping no one thinks I've been sent as spy or emissary. Feelings are raw in Berlin from the broken engagement.

"No one knows I'm here. I bought a one-way ticket."

I am treated to the Kafka glance, where he briefly directs the full force of his being at you, and then he laughs.

"My dear Miss Hannah, no one runs away to Prague. At least no one from Berlin. You are the first. Please accept a cup of coffee and a cheese bun, on behalf of a grateful populace, who are honored by your presence. Also some fruit."

I look longingly across the table at the sausage bun one of his friends is eating.

"Oscar's sausage is an insult to the digestive system," Franz says.

"You can't expect everyone to be like you and live on wood chips and birdseed," says another friend, Felix the philosopher. His eyebrows and mustache take too much command of his face in the manner of stage makeup which is meant to project to the back row but up close seems like clumsy artifice. None of the friends are handsome like Franz but they look different from the young men in Berlin. I notice how dear Franz chews his cheese bun, more thoroughly than seems necessary and with seriousness of purpose.

"I have a question for Miss Hannah," he says, but he's really addressing his friends. "Do you think I can reasonably expect a woman to share my life?"

He'd want a small cell and absolute quiet so he could write. And much of the time, of course, he'd want to be alone. Not even coming together for meals. His wife could slip food under his door.

"Maybe Felice might find it lonely but I wouldn't. Please let me stay with you. I could work in your father's store as a clerk."

More laughter, and the suggestion that Franz should take me up on this offer because working in his father's store, or any business enterprise, is one of the several Hells. The blockheaded father Kafka tries to drag dear Franz into the family businesses, tries to impart business love into his son.

"Dear Hannah," he says, "My reputation with your family is bad enough. We must see about getting you home."

And over my protests, Franz and his friends take me to the station, buy me a one-way ticket to Berlin, and wait to see that I board the train because dear Franz isn't going to take chances.

This time the rhythm of the train reminds me of him putting so much effort and attention into chewing his cheese bun, and the reference to wood chips and bird seed. He will never love me, not in the way I want, but for one afternoon I was part of his world. I met his closest friends and found them agreeable, saw for myself men who were not younger versions of my father.

I went back to Berlin but never went home.

I changed my name, cut off its tail, became Hannah Katz who lives in the alley.

The Muse

Late autumn, 1923. A million marks buys a postage stamp and the streets are full of the walking wounded. More crow than canary, I sing grand opera in mock Yiddish at the White Mouse Cabaret, where the line between da-da and ka-ka is invisible.

I dream of seeing dear Franz in the audience.

He's moved to Berlin.

He is living with a woman, Dora Dymant, a Chassidic rabbi's daughter from Poland. The soul of goodness, according to Max Brod, who says he's never seen his dearest friend so happy. I should see this happiness for myself. They love to entertain.

They live in a tiny apartment, the top floor of a semi-detached house in a quiet neighborhood. There is a park across the street.

She has a sweet face, this Dora, soft and unguarded

"Franz will be so happy to see you," she says as we climb the narrow staircase.

Until we reached the top he remains mine in the way that the star you choose to steer by is yours. He'd loved the Yiddish actors, how comfortable they were in their skin. Their irreverence.

Dora tells me he studies Hebrew.

Hebrew bought them together, his efforts to master the language and Dora's proficiency in it. Hebrew, and his kindness towards children. She'd worked in the Hebrew Children's Home, next to the seaside hotel where he took his vacation, and he used to visit. She believes him to be a tzadik, a holy man, a saint. One of the Lamed Vavnik, the thirty-six unknown righteous men, unknown even to themselves for whose sake God does not destroy the world.

"What about righteous women?"

I ask out of spite, not honest curiosity.

By way of response she says dear Franz is the only person in Berlin who shared the sense of everyday holiness that is second nature to the Chassidim. Why, the simple joy he took in eating a banana!

This visit was a mistake, but no turning back because just then dear Franz (hers, the saint) opens the door, a simple act that seems to take every ounce of his remaining strength. His skin is ashen, and that rattling cough.

If he is indeed one of the righteous thirty-six, I hope there's an understudy.

One room serves as kitchen, parlor and study. I notice a pile of papers in a corner by his desk. Worshipful Dora is not a meticulous housekeeper.

They are children playing house.

He drapes a dishtowel over one arm, and his exaggerated gestures are comic as he pulls out a dining chair for me.

"We must serve you tea, Miss Hannah. It will be good practice for when Dora and I open our café in Palestine."

"Don't forget about the dessert menu," Dora says.

"We have linzer torte, sacher torte, crème brulee, charlotte russe, and cherry-covered cheesecake. Dear one, bring out the pastry tray."

The pastry tray is a plate of dry brown biscuits of the sort commonly sold as digestive aids. I deliberate over my choices, ask if I could have more than one, and change my mind.

"What I really would prefer is a simple biscuit," I say, which delights them.

Yes, he is writing every day, he tells me, and then coughs.

"He writes letters to a little girl we met in the park who lost her doll," Dora says.

If this little girl is young enough to cry over a lost doll she is probably too young to have designs on dear Franz. She might, however have been a prostitute, of which Berlin has infinite varieties.

"Actually he's writing letters that the doll would write if it could. The doll is on a journey. She loves the little girl but she's curious about the world and needs to pursue her destiny," Dora says.

"Does she want to go to Palestine?" I ask.

Dora treats this as a serious question, says it would be out of character for this particular doll.

"I'm also writing a story about a singing mouse," says dear Franz. "Her name is Josephine."

Next he'd be writing nursery rhymes, this usurper. Dora's Franz.

My Franz was the least sentimental of writers. Gregor Samsa, commercial traveler, wakes up to discover he's turned into a giant cockroach. Joseph K. is brought before a tribunal and never told why so there's no possibility of defense. God is the sclerotic old man you must carry on your back who tries to choke you.

Dear Franz is happy. He is dying.

He wants me to tell him everything starting from what I ate for breakfast and the view outside my kitchen window.

The Muse

I was the first familiar face Dora recognized after she died, and she considers me her only friend. I remain dear to her on the strength of that short visit. Like many women who have had a Great Love, she likes to lord it over the rest of us, which hasn't made her popular, but she's the only one who tolerates my complaints.

Felice thinks I'm a fool not to appreciate eternity with its stable currency and superb dental care. She smiles all the time now, reveals a lovely set of white, well-formed teeth.

Kafka's Czech girlfriend, Milena the journalist, thinks I'm greedy for wanting more. She can be happy anywhere, even Ravensbrück, and the afterlife is an improvement from the camps. Clean water, and no rats. Husbands and lovers ache with unrequited love for the women they abused on earth. Milena's husband was spectacularly unkind. Now he works as a porter at one of the hotels and Milena pretends not to notice him.

"You'll soon feel different," she says, as if decades hadn't passed. As if we haven't had this same conversation many times. "There's nothing like that first apology from an abject lover. Haven't you seen Kurt?"

I have to laugh.

"I'm sure he has me confused with his second wife, the one who knit those awful sweaters, not the dancer."

Up here Kurt and I are old comrades with faulty memories. No trace of sexual frisson remains. He has a garden plot with a little hut at one end, just like you'd find in Germany on the outskirts of any large city. He says true happiness is the absence of desire.

In that case, true happiness leaves a lot to be desired.

Over coffee at the Café des Artistes, Dora and I talk, or rather she reminisces and I feed bits of sausage roll to the cats.

Did she ever tell me how much dear Franz appreciated the smallest things, right up to the end, even the ability to swallow water?

The cats at nearby Old Vienna are all black and white, while the ones who hang around our table are tabbies and calicos, plump kitchen cats. Dora says the tuxedo cats keep to themselves, just like Milena, Felice and even Grete Bloch. She thinks the others resent her out of jealousy.

The soft faced earnestness of her youth has given way to something more stylized, mature suffering complicated by formal dramatic training.

I remain amused that she sees no inherent conflict in worshipping dear

Franz as a higher spiritual being and expecting him to stick with the groundlings after death. Or expecting to ride into heaven on his coattails.

"Did you really expect God to save a place in heaven for a Lamed-Vavnik's girlfriend?" I ask her.

She corrects me in a low voice that carries.

"I was Kafka's Wife."

Heads turn in our direction.

"But you see my point."

"Which is, dear Hannah?"

Her smile is a glimpse of sun through otherwise heavy weather, and you can see the residual charm.

"He was a writer, not a saint, and you destroyed his work. Even my bourgeois cousin Felice knew the value of his letters."

"Our love was private. It was not meant for the world to peer at. You wouldn't understand, being from Berlin."

A small tuxedo cat approaches us, comes close enough to let me flirt with it. Our kitchen cats signal displeasure with flicks of their tails. The tuxedo cat pauses to lick a front paw, as though this was what it had in mind all along.

Those last nights in Berlin. No time for secrets or standing on ceremony.

"There should have been more than a few scratchy recordings to mark my time on earth," I say, which I've said before, but never with such bitterness.

"I saw you perform once," Dora says. "By then Franz was too weak to go out nights so he often sent me in his place."

"Oh, I was a joke in the beginning, just rude noise and nerve."

She reaches into the commodious hand bag that she carries with her at all times, a refugee habit, and hands me a book, the complete stories of Franz Kafka.

"Josephine and the Mouse People is on page 325. It's the story he was working on when you visited us."

"Forgive me, but I would prefer not to read children's stories by Kafka. Being from Berlin I'm not partial to whimsy."

"Then I'll read it for you," she says, and commences before I can stop her:

"Our singer is called Josephine. Anyone who has not heard her does not know the power of song."

Josephine doesn't exactly sing. It's something other than singing, a kind of piping, really, not unlike the sounds of ordinary mice, only presented to them as a great gift and received in grateful spirit. Their lives are hard. Physically vulnerable and surrounded by enmity, they rely on practical sense and cunning to survive in a hostile world. Ostjuden mice.

The Muse

The tiny stage. All of us together.

He'd made the best in me immortal. I wanted to give voice to our kind in dark times. Those of us with no aptitude for camouflage.

We who could only be ourselves.

"You were Josephine," Dora says. "Or rather, she was you."

The hunger that made me ruthless was gone. In its place was something I couldn't begin to describe. I hoped there were words for it in Yiddish.

Christina M. Rau

WOMEN AND MEN

Tonight the women
Will throw back their heads
Open their mouths wide
Will let their hair tangle twist
Will touch glasses to lips
Tip way back
Will kick up kick off
Will hoot holler squint
Swirl their dresses
And pounce on floors

Tonight the men
Will belly up to the bar
Open their mouths
Will throw down chips
Will scratch and slap
Nod nod nod
Will lean to one side
Will bite cigar tips
Untuck their shirts
And sing

George Drew

SIGHTINGS

1. Frank O'Hara in Saratoga Springs

Frank O'Hara is dead but he has not
collapsed, I'm not high on opium or weed
and the man I saw could have been Frank
O'Hara and as far as I'm concerned was
just sitting there at a sidewalk café
on where else but Broadway wolfing
down cheeseburgers and papaya juice and
groovin' on I'd say the cute little fillies hoofin'
by (except of course Frank O'Hara was gay)
and in his gaunt way was with his cropped
short and by then gone gray hair and
with his shirt sleeves rolled up in
a Fifties cool cat kind of way as handsome,
meaning that even if in fact because Frank
O'Hara's dead he couldn't have been and if
as it appeared he was merely a nostalgic pale
simulacrum likewise centered by the beauty Frank
O'Hara so famously proclaimed himself,
why then he as far as I'm concerned (except
of course Frank O'Hara was gay) was.

2. John Milton in Dunkin' Donuts

So there he was in his black suit and black hat
downing ten-ounce cups of what America runs on
and pondering the mystery of the long poetic line
as opposed to the shorter, something he felt all poets
ought to ponder, when out of nether regions
hundreds of strict verses came, each so formed

George Drew

and fast even Homer and Virgil wouldn't be
able to keep up, the prosody of suffering so perfect
it opposed his ever opening a poem with a muse
invoked. And so it was he gave up three-and four-
beat lines and exiled rhyme, subsisting on loose
pentameters, stanzas like paragraphs in drag,
and the antiseptic solace of forms more rigged
for Hell than Dante's hallucinogenic geography,
more than another blank-verse batch of creepy angels
holding court over a hellishly hot latte, Paradise
chilled to the chemical dependency of NutraSweet.

3. Charles Darwin in the Poestenkill Post Office

I hate it, the silver oxygen tank
tethered to him, its rubber monkey squeals
as it rolls along behind him over
the tiled Post Office lobby floor,
its rapid-fire compressed breaths.
I hate it, how he positions himself
next to me at the black counter
where I'm going through the mail
I don't want on this crisp September day,
all the while trying to believe that no
real news really is good news.
Under my breath I curse the monthly bills
and campaign flyers, my haul this day,
but he hears me and says something
about adapting. Nodding curtly I leave,
but all day I keep looking over my shoulder,
searching the colorful foliage of maple and birch,
wondering where in god's name the monkey is,
wondering what its angle of attack will be,
wondering when it will attach itself to me,
wondering how much fiddling it will take
to unleash what I know I can't.

Bradford Winters

Amateur Night at the Conscience Club

Look at you. All fucked up and nowhere
to go. Fugitive that you are in the wooden
crosshairs of a water gun, eyes
like quicksand between one thought
and the next. Big Sinner. Francis Ford
Mea Culpala. Mr. Historectomy.
Who once found it funny
Santa's anagram gives the gift
that keeps on giving, or fitting
that the brain is shaped like a maze.
Ha-ha. How fitting. That was then,
this is Mao. You still don't get it,
do you? You're like the guy
who comes home drunk and takes
a piss in the litter so as not to waste
all that water, then goes calling
his runaway cat in a downpour.
What am I going to do with you?
Or, for that matter, you with me?
At night, when I tuck my inner
child into bed, he looks up at me
with those eyes so deep and so blue
the submarines on his pajamas
glow like radar. No, I assure him,
I'm not going to destroy you.
Like that does any good. So he asks
for the Caravaggio, and I picture
the calling of St. Matthew at sundown
in the tavern. But I let him make
the same mistake his father first made,
which was to miss—I know, how is
this possible?—to miss that figure

Bradford Winters

pointing from the shadows at the edge
of the table, his finger limp enough
to hook the sunken head of a publican.
And missing it, to think the bad Italian
was even so inspired to place the Lord
just outside the bar, barely beyond
the canvas, as if that encounter
were as much if not more about the way
an open door, a doorway, admits the light.

The Air Around Her Objects *is part of an in-progress collection entitled* The True Outskirts of Home. *Each section (as experiment) contains a passage (as homage) from Marcel Proust's* The Guermantes Way *(Treharne).*

Jefferson Navicky

The Air Around Her Objects

ROBERT, WHO HAD RETURNED TO the city the preceding night, had promised to take me to Winslow Park, and although I had not mentioned it to him, I hoped that we might have lunch there. Instead he invited me to have lunch in a village restaurant south of the city with his mistress, whom we were to afterwards accompany to a rehearsal. We were to pick her up before noon, after leaving Winslow, at her house on the outskirts of the city.

I exchanged a few words with Justine. We cut across the village. The houses were sordid. But beside the most dilapidated of them, the ones that looked as if they had been scorched by a shower of sulfur, a mysterious shape stood, making its days along the faded street, a resplendent angel stretching the dazzling protection of its widespread wings in blossom: a pear tree. Robert walked ahead with me a little way and began to speak.

"If on a winter's night, a traveler who left Bowdoinham at the end of a day, night following him and turning with the bends of the road, were to glimpse the black branching wings of such a tree spread out against the deadened screen of darkness, he might not know its majesty. But upon rising in the morning and looking to the east, its pleasing form would be laced upon the golden screen of sunrise. How could this not bolster a traveler otherwise beset with melancholy at the difficulty of human interactions, indeed simple humanness, how could it not brighten him? He would neither know whose tree it was, nor would he care; he would neither know when, even if, it bore fruit, nor its exact age or height. The tree would simply etch itself onto his happiness. He wouldn't want to know its mysterious shade, not yet at least. A beautiful pear tree in a village."

Justine was so clumsy with her hands when she ate that one received the impression that she must appear extremely awkward onstage. She recovered her dexterity, I imagined, only when she was making love with the touchingly intuitive foresight of women who are so in love with men's bodies that they immediately sense what will give most pleasure to those bodies so different from their own. Did she allow such pleasure for herself, for her own body? Love often moves across body boundaries, pleasure to touch a duplicate, back and forth, back and forth. But just as often, and perhaps more, the pleasure only extends to one body, one love to the other's exclusion like a passenger on a train bound for Boston who is unable to look at the beauty of the countryside passing the window. Justine dropped her butter knife, thudding off the arm of her chair before clattering to the floor. She gave a little laugh as if she had expected it to happen. I reached down to pick it up. "It's a little curse of mine," she whispered as I handed it back to her and our hands brushed when I retracted and she took the knife.

I was told by old men whose memories went far back, and by young women who had heard it from these old men, that if women like Justine were socially exiled it was because of their extraordinary dissolute past, and when I objected that dissolute conduct was no obstacle to social success, they described her actions as something utterly in excess of anything to be met today. On the lips of those who told the tale, her misconduct became something so terrible I was hardly capable of imagining, something on a catastrophic scale belonging in the same category as public defecation or the defilement of a rose. And yet, when pushed to elaborate on the specifics of the offense, those taletellers demurred, saying it was too awful to retell. "Perhaps another time, young man, when I am not eating." Indeed this would prove to be challenging as the old man relating this particular story seemed to be perpetually caught in the moment of lifting liver pâté or a deviled egg to his lips.

    I couldn't stop seeing her as a shadow, my shadow. If the shadow is the body's representation, the silhouette is a representation of that representation. A silhouette is a good hole into which we throw light and dark, virtue and sin, the self and its double, the body and the soul. It was absence that most concerned me now. What was the shape of the air around her objects? How did whiteness swoop in to tuck itself against her figure? It was easy to see her form but to visualize her negative space was much more difficult. What was it that her arm extended into? The entirely worn fabric of the air. I'd come to accept that I would not know her silhouetted darkness, for no one can know another's night; it was the shapes around her, her white recesses and how she dwelled in them, that I would like to inhabit. I would like to breathe that air, and to discover into what ocean the air descends. She had suddenly restored to my keeping the thoughts, the shadows, and the souvenirs that I had thought lost to me. I could not have felt it with any more confidence. I was alone, but wanted to be with her—this woman who I'd thought so clumsy at first, who I thought even dull, and of course who was already spoken for by Robert, the person with whom I shared my closest friendship. The urge for her came on like a glove into which I did not even remember slipping my fingers. Soft, sorrowful fingers already incapable of tracing any other body besides the one silhouetted in my mind.

    Weary, resigned, with still several unquantifiable hours stretched in front of me, the grey day stitched away its pearly cloud line, and I was filled with the thought that I was to remain lacking close contact with her and with no more degree of acknowledgement between us than between two acquaintances who share a mutual friend. I had the urge to write her a letter containing the plenitude of her body and my desire to live in it like a bather walking towards the edge of a dock about to dive into deep water. Such a letter would be undeniable. It would be a letter full of distinct phrases coming together in better light, and full of music. Let Go Music, New Form Music, Roxy Music, not Happy Forget Me Music, but music that would roll her into me with a little burst of bass drum, a well placed riff, Devil Dive Music, Come Home Music, New School Music,

Old World Music. All of it in a letter in which, at its end and before my slanted signature, I would ask her to accompany me to a show at the Aphodian next week where a brilliant band would play all of the music mentioned above and to which we would dance all night, smelling each other's sweat amidst the stale blanket of beer and body odor.

Certainly it is more reasonable to devote one's life to women than to postage stamps, teapots, or even oil paintings and sculpture. Yet the collector's aesthetics do not pass unnoticed: the thrill of fully disclosed, unmitigated material desire; fine contours and shapely curves. There is nothing like desire to obstruct any resemblance between what one says and what one has on one's mind. Time presses, and yet it seems as though we are trying to gain time by speaking about things that are utterly alien to the one thing that preoccupies us. Robert invited me once again for lunch with Justine, this time along the seashore, breaking waves, but it was no longer the seashore that captivated my eye. It was to my heart that she spoke in her deadly way. Robert blurred in the background. It is not possible, in such a dangerous guise, to regard the kindling of the miracle as a thing to be desired. As I placed a cherry tomato between my teeth like a cat holds a beloved fingertip, I held it there for a moment, imagining it her nipple, before popping it with a sharp tick of my tooth, flesh and juice spreading throughout the deep ends of my mouth.

"What really worries me is that if we go on like this I may have to kiss you."

"What a lucky misfortune that would be."

I did not respond at once to this invitation. Another person might have found it superfluous, for Justine's way of pronouncing her words was so carnal and so soft that her speech alone was like a kiss. A word from her lips was a favor, and her conversation covered you in kisses.

Robert was away at a training near the border and Justine had startled me with a visit in the early afternoon. Her hands had, a moment prior, been spread palms up in front of me. I had told her of her life line, her love line, her Mount of Venus, the bands of luck, how her hands curl when opened from a fist.

She moved closer and began speaking words I no longer registered, only their soft flutter against my pain-body as if a flock of nameless mottled birds simultaneously took flight, battering me with their feathered wings. I could not remember a more euphoric discombobulation, a cascade of lips crossing my borders.

Her quiet circles. Her blossoming face. Her flushed valleys. Her dark surfaces. I spoke these locations to myself because I believed there was such a thing as knowledge through the lips. I told myself that I was to know the taste of this bodily rose, my mouth beginning to move toward the cheek I had envisioned, the exact field of plump taughtness I'd expected. Her talented neck. Drifting over the expanses in between and coming up against the clear barrier of the breastbone. But before my lips lose themselves, the turn of her nose. We kiss, our noses as ill-placed as extra appendages. I would love to follow hers as it sniffed along my crevices for faint perfumes. All possibilities, and a solid rotation of the body brings so many more, plump dimples up the spine, my lips crushed against cheeks and my eyes no longer see. Nothing except for the accelerating speed at which the experimental phenomenon of unknown origins—the body—continues to unfold, folds unfold and unfold. Into my own body I more fully take the taste I so desired, a shift in which I watch myself watching her body lying in the soft rumpled bed. I can no longer feel anything aside from the buzzing of my own body and from which I never want to rise—simply to stay in this slip until the horizon blurs into a meaningless ploy.

In between moments of constant thought, I walked. The Pine Loop, Marginal Way, out to the Head Light, along the cobblestones of the Old Port, down congested thoroughfares, up the Hill and down to the Eastern beach, a boat out to an island and along its perimeter, inside the pocked and pitted interiors, through the compliments received from others, the Crane Way, the Harrasseeket Loop, beyond the usual ambit of the known walks, to the State Pier where I drank bubble tea, to Long Wharf where I conversed with colleagues, seldom the most direct route, past the morning newspapers shouting at me, the longshoremen and the shop windows. I was pained by signs of affection, but what hurt most to see was that there were unhappy people in almost every house I passed. I wanted, more than anything, to utter the words "I am no longer in love," but I couldn't. I imposed all that movement upon myself, and yet the feeling was still there, tucked away into some inaccessible corner, refusing to make any gesture of availability and also refusing to show any signs of abatement.

Certain women are incompatible without the double bed in which we find appeasement at their side, whereas others, to be caressed with a more secret intention, need leaves blown by the wind, the sound of water in the dark, things as ephemeral and evasive as they are. I walked among such leaves, the season's first to fall. So surprising to notice a few golden leaves scattered across one's path. The air too possessed an ending chill. At this moment of the year, it is, and has always been, impossible for me to feel optimistic; happy in isolated moments, yes, but not ever settled in the overarching turning, like a man who has just begun his afternoon walk at sunset. I had convinced myself, and indeed now it was too late to believe otherwise, that I was in love with Justine, this temperamental girl, my best friend's lover, someone, I suspected, who would have no qualms about shattering my paradoxical hope at a moment's notice. Hope? Was it that? Lust? Did I simply want to destroy myself? Whatever it once was had now taken on the tinge of early autumn, one or two leaves littered on the ground beneath an otherwise lush canopy, and around the edges of leaf, of stem and of self, I felt a sharp intruding nip, the sensation of falling and a drop in temperature.

Then the sun disappeared and the mist became denser in the afternoon. Darkness fell early, and I dressed for the evening, but it was still too soon to leave the house; I decided to send a car for Justine. It felt like the only thing to do. I was reluctant to ride in the car myself, not wishing to force my company upon her during the journey, so instead I sent a note with the driver to ask whether I might come meet her. I watched the car pull away, and knew the outcome of the evening would not be positive for me, but I was resolved, like a doctor about to begin a futile surgery, to set the process in motion. About forty minutes later, the driver returned and handed me a note on pink paper, scrolled and tied with a black ribbon. I observed myself pull the ribbon's knot and unroll the note. It began "Dear A----" and continued in four swift sentences to proclaim that she no longer wished to see me in social or intimate settings. "This has never been a wise decision," like it was a casual investment in petty stock, "I'm sure you'll agree, one that need not be mentioned to Robert." She then said she was leaving that evening for New York and would be there for two months, working as an artist's assistant. "Please don't bother trying to contact me there. Fondly," like a knife, "Justine."

I re-rolled the note, tied on the black ribbon and gave the note back to the driver, asking him to dispose of it. I had no other choice than to go out into the night to walk.

The Air Around Her Objects

It was surprisingly restful to listen to Justine's speech floating across and through the mild cacophony of voices in the reception hall. Her voice possessed the eerily perspicacious quality that could find me within the densest wall of sound. Expressing some slight thing of the moment, it was singularly pointed, as if I was alone in her company and she condescended and clarified the melody of her speech to the point of an old song on the record player, a warbling soprano, the crackling of the arm's needle and dust. Then, as I risked a sidelong glance at Justine, I could see, calmly imprisoned in the unending afternoon of her eyes, an expanse of sky above an island in the bay, bluish, thin and slanted at the same angle of incline as Robert's eyes. Indeed she was speaking of him, one of his recent accomplishments, in the breathless, idiot manner of touching idolatry, a blanketing love as evident as gravity. I could never tune out her voice. Exiting through the kitchen, walking between waiters and the smell of seared meat, I left the crowded air, knowing that I would not return.

WINNER OF THE KNIGHTVILLE POETRY CONTEST

William Derge

A RED CHAIR

In De Hooch's *Interior*, that little girl with the whip is not real.
She is the ghost of the mistress's childhood.
Just look at how she's stuck like a decal on the canvas.
Despite all that baby fat, she has no weight.
Look how her face resembles the printed face of a paper doll.

A closer look reveals that the whip is a fishing pole.
She has been fishing in the *Kloveniersburgwal*.
But she's still the ghost. Even the dog looks away.
Actually, I think, while fishing, she fell into the canal,
and the messenger is about to inform the mistress
that she had drowned in childhood.

And so, as it turns out, it is the mistress who is not real.
She has not existed for all these years.
She has been an illusion to herself.
Should she listen to the call of her childhood's self,
who is not quite real herself, and shoo the little puppy off her lap?
Should she go to the door and walk into the bright Dutch exterior,
where the canal runs the length of the street?

Of course, she can choose to stay; God will permit her to go on,
but now with the knowledge that there is nothing beyond
this illusion of life for her; no meaning,
no purpose, no judgment and redemption.
And the little girl—the ghost of her childhood—is waiting;
she is waiting, and she is mad, mad as hell,
because her little fishing pole was never meant to catch anything.

A Red Chair

How one aches to see the messenger poised with the message,
the eyes of the mistress knowing something's up.
How one aches to know that all this Dutch contentment and domesticity
is about to go out the artfully leaded window in the center of the painting,
on whose frame the artist, de Hooch, has cleverly carved his name in paint.

In the midst of all this tension stands an empty red chair,
from which light seems to emanate,
as if the chair were the source of the room's dim illumination.
Solid and stationary, bright and charged with presence,
it eventually becomes to the shifting eye, the center of this closed Dutch interior.
And the little girl, the mistress and the messenger share
in its light, its color, its design and utility. There is a rightness to this,
just as there is a rightness to those two old men across the canal
with their paunches and watches.

It is summer, after all.
The windows are open to the warm air, which,
though invisible, is somehow felt to be present in the painting.
Presumably, there are fish in the canal to be caught.
People dress lightly, yet still fashionably.
The floors are incredibly clean.
Everything in this Dutch interior is incredibly clean.

We are reminded by the reality of this red chair, then,
that the figures in the painting have an existence separate from the artist's,
and that, though he may have preserved them for some time
(though certainly not for eternity),
they have successfully eluded his complete possession of them,
and as they are not his property, they are equally not ours.

So, at any moment of her choosing, the mistress might decline to open the message,
the messenger may become overwhelmed with pity
and walk out into the sunlight feeling that if he died at that moment
or soon after, he would be guaranteed a place in eternity,
even the old men across the canal may come over and make some concourse
with the figures in the interior setting.

William Derge

And the darkness of evening will come and overtake them all,
making first its broad signature on the red chair,
then, on the dogs and the mistress.
The messenger will be long gone, alone in a tavern
drinking away his sorrow or feeding his contentment.
The old men will have put away their business in a drawer.
And the frightening little girl with the fishing pole
will have disappeared or simply come inside and gone to bed.

James K. Zimmerman

Creation: The Madlib Version

When (He/She/It/They) (was/were/might've been/could be) just a (wee little/overbearing/arrogant/cutesy poo) young omni-(present/potent/scient/vorous) (being/oneness/nothingness/postal clerk), (He/She/It/They) decided to create a (science experiment/terrarium/new world/biosphere) in the back yard. In a (fishbowl/crockpot/magnetized vortex/pigsty), (He/She/It/They) (piled/glued/spat/shoveled) primordial soup (mama's recipe), mud, DNA helices, salt, and just enough water to cover; then (He/She/It/They) turned up the heat to (simmer/explode/apocalypse/sexed up), being careful not to (deep fry/incinerate/agglutinate/excoriate) the mix too much. Just as the mixture was starting to (coalesce/degenerate/genuflect/cremate), (He/She/It/They)'s (mother/father/car salesman/softball coach) called, and (He/She/It/They) left to go (have dinner/destroy a future galaxy/create a new dimension/wash up). The (glob/pestilence/Eden/carbuncle) in the back yard continued to (regress/digress/evolve/evacuate) for what seemed like (a week/a dog's age/untold millennia/until 4004 BC), moving quickly through the (Cretaceous/Crustacean/Creationist/Cartoonist) eras into what we now call (modern times/postmodern times/now/what the?). (He/She/It/They), now a (full-grown/decrepit/little-known/sweet-as-pie) old (being/oneness/nothingness/bank teller), suddenly remembered the (train wreck/hi-tech/debacle/oobleck) in the back yard, and returned to (examine/inhale/destroy/adore) it. To (He/She/It/They)'s (delight/dismay/disgust/dismemberment), (He/She/It/They) discovered that we had made heaven on earth, thrown the beer cans in the flower bed, smoked the brains out of the atmosphere, created reality TV, cured atheism, and peed in the pool. And (He/She/It/They) declared it was (Good/revolting/unconscionable/freakin' awesome).

The (End/Beginning/Transition/Transmogrification).

Cary Waterman

Disambiguation

> *Disambiguation pages are not intended for games of "free association."*
> *Please use them carefully and only when needed.* —mozilla.org

In last light   a radiance   of cardinals
eleven and more   coming from the sunset

all of them princes   calling   pur dy
                         pur dy   pur dy
      servants   of the servants   of God

intentional links and   wings low & steady
       redirecting across the small backyard

to choose   a new prince   apostle of gold safflower seeds

like the garlands of safflowers found in the tomb of Tutankhamun

a kind of double disambiguity which is extremely rare

they are a long way from Northern Canada
       where many Cree and Metis are descended

from a Vatican of cardinals who appeared on their horizon in 1780
reproduced prolifically
               trapping furs and converts
a set of specific type that shared the same   *(or similar)*   *name*

Cary Waterman

and provided a cardinal direction   or cardinal mark
ex cathedra   N S E and, most intuitively, W
         the dead reckoning
not a search where there is no significant risk
                                         of confusion

because the dead want to say something
       about   cardinals   about ambiguity

that you can always go back   and   modify

your errors   which are cumulative
       and grow larger with time

like truth for example   or   words

that do not point to a single meaning
       from the list of   meanings
but to yet another   disambiguation

which is not the way cardinals navigate

allowing a traveler   to choose
and a code of honor to fix all
       resulting   misdirections

from the trees down   from the ground up
       enduring missiles   knowing the path
a destination guide of their own
       position of stars and earth's magnetic field

as in   this path   this rock   this golden seed
       this kingdom of relations.

Elinor Benedict

Early Girl

Some tomato! yelled whistling GIs on furlough
when spotting a girl in shorts that bared what they called
great gams—silky bronze legs that led to whatever

helped those guys stop seeing dozens of tanks wallowing
in snow, mud, fire, blood, gristle—all that stuff
that killed their dreams of warm sheets. But what

did I know then, sub-teen early as this small tomato plant
I now stuff into dirt, my legs creaking, white hair flying in chill
wind, while new wars blow hot, and girls are called what-

ever stops men's mouths from screaming. So when the names
of real tomatoes—Big Boy, Beefmaster, Better Bush—
shoot me back to the Forties, I buy Early Girl for what

cold climate needs and memory wants to play with, because
this girl's not coming back, the one whose daddy didn't whistle,
but loved red tomatoes and made bombs for peace. So what

am I doing to myself as I see-saw between early and late,
men and women, life and death, war and peace—trying
to balance while I add manure, hope for sun, and wonder what

it's all for. Is someone watching a movie of me as I grow
up and old, someone who loves me enough to let me keep
living a while longer until I love myself? And what

comes next, Mrs. Tomato, either miraculous little globe or
bright-eyed, black-haired girl with trowel in the old picture frame?
One to be eaten, the other still asking why, how, what.

Erica Plouffe Lazure

THE COLD FRONT

WHEN WE SAW JOAN SMALLS, she was standing on the lip of her unshoveled driveway off Strutmore Road, howling as she removed what was left of her long underwear. It was the day after a blizzard, a Saturday; by the time we got there, she wore nothing but her snow boots. She screeched at her husband Curtis about "Swiss Miss snow bunnies" and "slutty Barbie dolls." She hurled many snowballs. She cursed, loudly. When we turned down the radio, we caught "that nasty e-mail-sending whore" and "why won't you just listen?" Curtis Smalls was silent. He shoveled snow.

We were out for a ride with the kids after the storm, test-driving the four-wheel drive on Lora's Jeep, when we came across the Smalls. I slowed down and flipped up the shade attachment for my glasses to get the full effect.

The Cold Front

"Lookit there, honey. A snow queen," I said. I have to admit, Mrs. Smalls looked pretty darn good. The cool air had hardened her nipples to a deep pink and you could almost see every last goose bump on her muscular body. Her hair was flyaway blonde, strewn skyward from static. Along with scattered stacks of magazines—was that a *Playboy*?—which blew about in the wind, her clothes littered the frozen lawn. I rolled down the window.

"James, don't," Lora said. She clutched the sleeve of my parka. "The kids!" I ignored her and stuck my head out the window.

"Hey, is everything all right there?" I asked. "You need any help?"

Mrs. Smalls turned toward us—no shame, only anger—and hurled a snowball in our direction. "Haven't you seen a naked woman before?" she yelled. "Get the hell out of here!"

"I don't think the Smalls need our help, dear," I said to Lora, trying to keep a straight face behind my beard.

"This isn't funny, James. I'm calling the police. We can't have this in our neighborhood," Lora said. She glanced back at Susie and Paul, asleep in their car seats. I followed her gaze and lowered my voice.

"Give her a break, Lora. There's a time when you'd have stripped down to your skivvies yourself just to make a point," I said. As it was, Lora had been wearing the same grey sweatpants and duck boots for three days. Her navy blue vest puffed up and distorted her top half. And you'd never guess that under her L.L. Bean look, a tattoo of blue stars lined the upper ridge of her hipbones, or that she used to strut around Duck's Tavern on a Thursday night singing karaoke in tight jeans and a tube top.

"That time is over," Lora said. She pawed through her purse for her cell phone.

Joanie Smalls had begun to stomp on magazines—*Playboy* and *Hustler* among them—as Curtis continued to shovel, his wide face expressionless. For a while, he used to anesthetize patients down at Mewborn Memorial. I would see him walking through the hospital from time to time when Lora was getting her chemo treatments, and he'd flash an icy smile, as neighbors do, and continue on his way. Then I heard down at Duck's that not long after they fired him from the hospital, he got into some online porn business. No one at Duck's knew why he'd been fired, but honestly I just couldn't imagine his thick fingers sticking needles into people on an operating table any more than I could see him selling porn out of his basement. He seemed too numb. Even now, he did not react to his wife's snowballs, or her accusations, not even when she yanked the shovel from his grip, pushed him down in the snow, straddled his stomach, and shook him by the collar of his coat, screaming, "I just want you to see me!"

Lora focused on her phone, thumbs pushing buttons. "No service," she said. "Damn."

"Put that phone away. Can't you see they're having it out?" I said, pulling out of neutral. I'd seen all I had to after that straddle maneuver. "Let's get out of here."

As soon as we got home, Lora stepped out of the Jeep with the phone pressed to her ear and headed indoors. The kids were awake now and fidgeting, so I took them out of their car seats and let them loose in the front yard. Susie followed her mother, while Paul went to check on the snowman we'd built that morning. It was almost time for dinner, but I didn't feel like going in the house. Instead I found my flask under the front seat of my truck, took a quick swig, and stowed it in my pocket as I joined Paul before the snowman.

Our snowman is an ordinary snowman. He's got an ugly blue scarf wound around his neck and an old Burger King crown on his head. He's sloppy-dumpy, like any other front yard suburban snowman, with charcoal features and an unpeeled carrot for a nose. I won't waste briquettes on buttons, or break branches for arms. It doesn't matter, really. In the end, arms or no arms, top hat or paper crown, all snowmen will eventually look alike: frozen and sagging into the grass, one big puddling mess.

I'd promised Paul earlier we could build another snowman—this time, a girl—before the snow melted.

"Then we'll have the set," I'd said. "A snowman. And a snow ma'am." I was in high school the last time a snowstorm like this blew through Mewborn, so I figured Paul and Susie and I could make the best of it. We'd even made a last-minute bread-and-milk run to the Food Lion on Highway Eleven, and watched the idling plow trucks.

"What do you think?" I said. "Time we get that snow ma'am underway?" Paul nodded.

Together we started to push snow into a mound. I could feel the chill of the air through my clothes and contemplated what it would be like to wear none. I took off my gloves and scooped snow into my hands. In a moment, my palms went numb and I thought about Joanie Smalls. What was she feeling out there? God, she looked amazing. Why did she strip like that? I contemplated this until I spied Paul's blue mittens on the ground next to me. I shook the slush out of my hands, then his.

"Come here, silly," I said. I wiped his hands on the cuff of my pants, then

The Cold Front

retrieved his mittens. The front door slammed. Lora and Susie were walking toward us. Lora's brows formed a prim double arch over her wide, blue eyes. She keeps her hair cropped short, even though she stopped chemo almost three years ago.

"What is your problem?" she said.

"Paul took off his mittens," I said. I wiped the last of the wet on my coat. "I'm just getting them back on."

"That's not what I meant," she said. "You know dinner will be ready soon."

"It will be too dark for snowmen after dinner," I said. I tugged at each of Paul's mitten cuffs, for emphasis. We were building a snowman. "This won't take long."

I helped Paul scoop more snow with my shovel. He patted it down with his mittened hands. Lora stood there, brimming with unspoken words. I let it ride.

"Don't you want to know what the cops said?" she finally asked.

"Not particularly," I said.

"Well, they're busy with calls from the snowstorm, but Sheriff Stanton said they'd send someone by," she said. "You know, to check."

"So someone can't be naked around here without you calling the sheriff, is that it?" I asked.

Paul started to form what looked like a huge snowball for the midsection. I set down the shovel, found my flask, and took another sip.

"Curtis Smalls is a pervert," Lora said. "His wife's no better. Indecent exposure in a snowstorm? Seriously. What's she trying to prove?"

"Who knows? You hardly know them," I said. I helped Paul roll the midsection onto the base. "I don't see why we got to get in on the tit patrol in the middle of nowhere. Getting mucked in their mess sure as hell won't solve ours."

"What does that mean, exactly?" Lora asked.

I stopped helping Paul and leaned on my shovel. "What I'm saying is, the Smalls' problems are not ours. And we got plenty of our own," I said.

"Well, you make a lot of sense," Lora said. She was trying to keep her voice low, but the heat loomed in her words. She grabbed my arm and dragged me away from the kids. "Some naked bimbo starts screaming at her porno pimp husband in the middle of a snowstorm, and you blame me for their problems and ours?"

"God, Lora. Don't put words in my mouth," I said. "I don't blame you for…"

"Nothing would be solved, you know, if I got buck naked in front of the world," she said.

I lowered my voice and moved in closer to her. "I wish you could hear yourself talk, Lora. Because seeing any part of you naked might do the trick," I said. "You haven't let me touch you, let alone fuck you, for how long?" She looked away, toward the kids, her arms folded across her chest.

"I'm just speaking the truth," I said. "I feel like I'm still paying for a two-year-old mistake."

Lora exhaled what was left in her lungs, unable to meet my gaze. Then she met me, full-faced. "You are," she said, grabbing hold of a branch as she walked away. When she let go, the snow from the branch came down over me in powdery chunks. Susie ran toward the backyard. As Lora tracked after our girl, I walked over to Paul and helped him finish the snowman's head.

The truth is, two years of no sex was a generous estimate. After Lora's operation, we tried once. It was a few months after her mother left and she was done with the chest packs and the painkillers and the drain tubes, after she decided she'd rather put the kids through college than pay for breast reconstruction. She said she felt ready. She said she wanted me. And I knew she'd be changed; I knew she'd have no breasts. But nothing prepared me for when our bodies actually touched. In the dark and through her nightgown, I pulled my hand away from her body. It was a reflex, involuntary, and clumsy, but she left our bed and nothing would convince her to come back. And I haven't touched her since. After that, she surrounded herself with the kids and made it so we never got a moment alone. She usually sleeps in Susie's room, or dozes on the couch; I go out to Duck's most nights to forget about it, and come home so late that it doesn't matter where we sleep. Apologies make it worse: Sorry for touching her. Sorry for pulling away. Sorry for the cancer. Sorry, now, for mentioning it.

Paul turned toward me and giggled.

"Daddy, you look like a snowman," he said.

"Thank you," I said, looking back at where Lora had been. "Say, you got a carrot on you? I can't smell a darn thing."

"She needs eyes," Paul said.

"How right you are," I said.

I went into the garage for the bag of charcoal and dug out a few coals and handed them to Paul. Then I broke the first snowman's carrot in two. As I watched Paul wedge each coal into the snowman's face and place the half carrot for its nose, I couldn't help but imagine that Joanie Smalls would probably want a guy like me. Someone who'd pay attention to her, like she wanted. Maybe she'd lean in a cheesecake pose on the hood of my truck. Or she'd sit on a fur skin rug in the snow, her hair in two braids brushing each breast, her knees bent, each heel touching the lower corners of the rug, letting me see the pink folds beyond her

The Cold Front

dark down. Her boots would still be on, and we'd make love right there, in front of the snowman. Or in front of her husband, who would continue to shovel, no matter what. And everything I'd ever felt would pour into her. And she would take in all of me, accept me completely with her eyes open, wanting more.

"Daddy? How do we tell it's a girl?"

"How do we tell who's a girl?" I said, face reddening.

"You said she's a snow ma'am," he said, emphasizing the "ma'am."

"So I did. Hold on," I said. I returned to the garage to find a few ribbons in the Christmas box that I had yet to bring to the attic. I pushed past last month's ceramic fir trees and gilded stars and ratty red stockings and focused on finding ribbons. Ribbons in hand, I returned.

"Here," I said, handing him the ribbons. "Put them on her head. Then we'll know."

Paul grinned as he took them. Leaning on my shovel, I watched him wrap the ribbons, green and gold, around her head.

"She's beautiful," I said. When he was done, Paul grabbed my hand and led me toward Lora and Susie, who were walking toward the front yard.

"Mommy, we made a lady out of snow!" Paul said.

Lora gave me a sharp look. Then, in a phony, loving-mother voice, she said, "A girl snowman. That's great, sweetie. Now whose idea was that?"

"Daddy's. He said it's a snow ma'am," Paul said.

"We've got the happy pair right on the lawn if you want to see them," I said. "Mister and missus." I sounded, for Paul's sake, friendly and upbeat. Like a guy who eats cereal for breakfast every morning.

"Well, I thought it was just a plain old snowman," Lora said.

"No, it's a girl," he said. "There's ribbons."

"Let's go see," she said, still looking at me, her eyes sending out all the reformed whore, fake church-lady meanness they could muster. As we approached the snow ma'am, I said, "Now, Lora. Don't you go calling the cops. I can assure you the snow ma'am is fully clothed."

It would have been one thing if Lora had just slapped me or called me an asshole in front of the kids, then went into the house. I would have preferred that. But instead she formed two scoops from the snow ma'am's midsection, held them to her chest, and said, "I'm sure you know exactly where to put these, James." Then she threw them both at me, dead-on.

The children giggled.

"Mommy hit Daddy with a snowball," said Paul, and Susie threw a handful of snow at Paul and soon they were romping and laughing, snow flying everywhere, as Lora and I stood there, arms crossed, glaring at each other.

I turned away from her, eventually, and as I did, the snowman's expression caught my eye. It looked to me just then like the charcoal had been arranged so the snowman held a smirking, leering grin. As though the snowman found Lora's snowball stunt extremely funny.

I reached for the shovel and sideswiped the snowman's head. His head hit the snow ma'am's straight on, and her head toppled, too. Lora backed away, and I ignored Paul's wails for me to stop. I'm ashamed to admit that I couldn't stop pummeling the snow-torsos with my fists. I stomped on their heads as my family retreated to the house. Bows and charcoal smiles and the paper crown and split carrots and scarf scattered across the lawn.

"Why do you have to ruin everything?" Lora said.

It was only then that I realized I was alone on the lawn. Lora had got the kids inside the house, away from me. I pounded on the door, my house key useless, thanks to the deadbolt.

"Why can't you see I'm sorry?" I yelled. I jiggled the doorknob one last time before I walked toward my truck. "I'm sorry!"

On my way I saw a lump of coal uncrushed from the snowman's grin. I kicked it. I kicked it again. It skittered down the driveway. I looked up at the darkening sky. What I really needed was to go for a drive.

I spent the next few hours rumbling down the back roads of Mewborn. We never see this much snow in eastern Carolina, and usually it shuts down nearly everything, especially where we live, some five miles out in the county. But the roads were mostly clear. Eventually I got the courage to return to Strutmore Drive. The Smalls' house was dark, save for a dim red light from a window on the second floor. Curtis's Yugo was gone from the driveway; Joanie's Camry remained.

I drove by a few more times before I stopped the truck on the side of the road. I rolled down the window to feel the night air on my face, sipping my flask. I idled there a long time, staring at footprint pock marks on the frozen, bare lawn, the shoveled driveway. I tried to imagine Joanie Smalls somewhere in that house, alone now, warm in pajamas, too brave for her own good. Then I thought of Lora, policing the neighborhood. I guess if someone drove by and saw me beating on a snowman with a shovel, she'd call the sheriff, too. And I'd deserve it. I tried to recreate my snow queen fantasy from this afternoon, but instead my mind kept drifting back to Lora, who was probably by now asleep on the couch or on the recliner in Susie's room. The last image that came to my mind as I drifted off was of me asleep in Lora's arms. When I awoke a couple hours later, the truck engine was still on, and I had just enough gas to get me back to the house. The light at the Smalls' had been turned off. I popped the truck into gear and drove home.

When I pulled into the driveway, I saw the wind had carried one of Paul's ribbons nearly to the road. I chased it down and wrapped it around my neck as I walked toward the house. The remains of our snow people lay in heaps on the front yard. I stood among the mess in the dark, thinking about Paul and Susie and Lora. I knelt down and began to gather the snow in a mound. Soon I'd shaped it into a snowman. Then I made another, and another. Soon there was a small village on the front lawn: icy, three-plop replicas, a dozen of them forming a small army, cold and sturdy in the moonlight.

By the time I finished, my knuckles were scraped and frozen, fingers numb. I was sweaty. It was then Lora joined me outside, in her blue vest, the cuffs of her pajamas pants tucked into her duck boots. She picked up a gold ribbon, shook it off, and wrapped it crisscross around the head of the snow person nearest the house.

"Why don't you come inside?" she said.

"I'm not done here," I said. That was true. I still had to pat down the base I was working on, make it concave, like a platter ready to receive the midsection.

"Let me help you," she said. She picked up the charcoal bag and began to place eyes on ice. She made black, three-point smiles on the frozen men.

"I'm fine here," I said.

"James," she said, "you're not fine."

I stood up. "Look. I don't give a shit about the cancer. And you always have to be so, so fucking proud or something. So perfect. All the time. And I'm just…"

Lora looked out at the lawn, as though she was searching for something. I stopped making the torso to look, too, to see what she saw. The lawn was dark and muddy in the spaces between the snowmen. It looked like there was no ground beneath them, and each one was fixed and frozen in its own world, floating in space in the darkness.

She approached one snowman and broke off a section of its head, forming it into a ball. Cupping her hands with care, she threw the snowball into the night.

"It's enough," she said. She made and threw another snowball, then turned toward me. "You're enough, all right?"

She moved to another snowman and scooped out another snowball.

"Cut it out, Lora," I said, annoyed that she'd hacked the snowman's head like that.

This time, she aimed for me. I ducked.

"You're getting snow everywhere," I said, even though I knew I sounded like an old lady. Snow got down my neck and stuck in my beard. "I'm warning you," I added in a tone I usually save for the kids.

"What'll happen?" said Lora.

She was holding a pair of snowballs at chest level. Crouching behind one of the snowmen, I stole a snowball from its middle.

"All, I'm saying is, you'd better watch it," I said. I hurled a snowball at her. It missed. I tossed three more, but only one nicked her vest. I threw another round her way, maneuvering through the yard, trying to avoid Lora's barrage, until we'd dismantled all the snowmen. Only one remained for each of us. I took the flask from my coat and took a swig.

"Any left in that for me?" Lora asked. She threw another snowball. It hit my chest, dead-on. She advanced toward me like a stealthy soldier, shielding herself.

"Not if you're my enemy," I said. I peeked over the icy midsection of mine, clutching my flask; Lora emerged from behind her snowman to face me. I stood and extended the flask in her direction. She took a sip, then tucked the flask into the pocket of her vest. I stepped closer to her. She sighed and stared at the sky.

I wanted to follow her upward gaze, but decided against it. Taking a breath, I reached toward her instead and rested my palm on her down chest, over her heart. She placed her hand over mine, and we stood together in the cold amidst our toppled bodies.

Thoreau Raymond

CANCER

Look at you sitting there. Cute and self-contained,
Just a mewling ball of fluff, weak, defenseless, all milk
teeth and dew claws, something to hold close and cuddle.

I took you in, sheltered you in the cradle of my pelvis.
Like a fetus in the womb, you slept, fed, woke. A tickle
under the rib cage, a twinge in the groin, a vague familiar

quickening. Your eyes unblinking as if waiting for a sign,
the light changing from red to green, stop to go.
You sashay through the reedy viscera, the glistening

loops of bowel. All slink, swagger and twitch of tail
as if to say, *I-know-who's-boss-and-so-should-you*.
You rub your whiskered chin against the luxurious heft

of liver. Purr in synch with the unsuspecting bellows
of my lungs, the lub-dub-dub of my trusting heart.
You sniff indignantly at a kidney, leave it for later.

Cock a slender paw to swat an ovary just because
it entices like a blown glass ball catching light.
A two-year old, you call everything you touch, *Mine*.

You bear no forethought, no malice. Hindquarters
tense with the kill. You pounce, wrap yourself around
brain, breast, bladder, bone. Dig in.

Matt Miller

Still Falling

The dark is the burlap
bagging your head
in hot breath hard
to breathe with that rope
around your throat
and then the floor quits
and you gasp for the slack
to cut out but there's nothing
but the dark and a breeze
between your knees
and you're still falling
through all your seams
those things you didn't do
with that girl who smiled
from the other escalator
the son you wouldn't have
the book you couldn't write
the tree you didn't climb
in Levine's yard even
if your little brother did
but you're still falling
wintering really down
and down and bored
with it all you decide
to learn French the fiddle
when to nine iron
and when to wedge
how it feels to be faithful
to your wife how it feels
to not be how much sugar
Kool-Aid needs when to tear
down the tree house

Still Falling

they never used and that
the universe is flat
and still falling no stopping
no sudden crackle spit
and wiggle so you drop
into thought for a thousand
years give or take a yo-yo's
length of string realizing
it's easy to be a holy man
at the working end of a noose
while your hood slips
off into a lilac evening
and you work out the math
for why the universe is
flat why umpires believe
the bat, why that smile
became your wife why
your kids still think to call
why Kool-Aid is the greatest
compliment you can give
to sugar and why the breeze
between your knees is warm
without the devil and when
you do come down to this
when you do see the summer
finally curling pink
upon the waves
you'll know the rest
will be a snap.

Bill Roorbach

Windflower

I'M GOING OUT TO SIT ON A ROCK. Because tomorrow is Mother's Day, a "holiday" Mom never had much use for. I called home one recent year, in fact—this was after her heart attack—and said the usual bright "Happy Mother's Day." And she only said (all gravelly and distracted and cross): "You're too *late*."

I head down into our woods briskly, and down into my neighbor's flood-plain fields. Here in Farmington, Maine, we've had almost four inches of rain in two days, and I can hear Temple Stream already. Our gentle stream! Roaring! The normally merely damp swale in the lower field is a rushing brook now, and I leap not quite across it with a splash, recall the wet-sneaker springtimes of my childhood. I've got mud boots, now, and push on, but my hike is going to be interrupted anyway: the stream has risen out of its banks, my daily route under several feet of coursing chocolate water. I stand at the fringe of the freshet up to the ankles of my boots and watch all the action—logs tumbling past, resolute alders diving and holding on, clouds scudding uncharacteristically northward, whitewater in the thalweg that is our stream. I'm energized, feeling fierce, still wrung out from all the crying overnight, crapulous from the whiskey I drank with friends instead of eating dinner. She's been dead not quite a month, and I'm just realizing how hard it's going to get now that the shock has worn off and reality sets in. My friends have all lost parents too: good talk. Here I am fifty-two and hung over like a college kid and leaping puddles like a little boy and missing my *mommy*. That's the word I keep hearing in my head: *Mommy*.

And now I can't get to my rock, which is up in the woods atop a glacial tumulus on the other side of what's supposed to be a little brook feeding our modest stream but is now a torrent feeding a sloshing, roiling, downhill pond where whitewater meets the flats. I slog my way back up to our woods and along high ground to another of my spots, what I call the thinking place, a sturdy little bluff above Temple Stream where it continues its push through the flats, a bedrock rise across from my neighbor's further fields, a good rock to sit on, not the one I'd planned, but. The water has dropped about two feet from its overnight crest, it appears, which must have come this morning very early: the rain quit at midnight or so. The incipient grasses and sedges on the high bank are all smoothed like hair combed with spit before church. The stream has gleaned last fall's dead stalks, and everything looks tidy. A perfectly barked, branched log—most of a really big tree—has risen and floated for the fourth time in two years, has made a hundred yards in that period, maybe ten overnight. At my feet the vernal-eternal flowers are up, bluets so sweet and tiny, called Quaker ladies by the settlers, and they do congregate, and they are dressed their best, and I think of mourners, can't help it. The forest floor is all trout-lily leaves, singular presences proud with drooping yellow flowers. Sessile-leaf bellwort I know, a great favorite, *Uvularia sessifolia*.

But I can't remember the one with the three whorled and divided leaves. Like many of the little flowering plants covering the forest floor today, it's a spring ephemeral, will rise only briefly before the canopy leafs out and blocks the sun. In a few weeks there will be no trace on the surface. I can still see it in Mom's hand these forty-five years later, can almost hear its name on her lips. We'd press such things in wax paper, make a delicate collection, learn the names. But this one I've forgotten. I get my *Newcomb's Wildflower Guide* out of my new fanny pack ("lumbar" pack, the cautious manufacturer calls it), work my way into the five-question key (leaves entire or divided?), but I am distracted by a familiar warbler melody: Wilson's warbler. As for the flower, I still can't get it. I'll have to ask Mom.

No. Oh, no. Can't do that. I'm on my own now with the wildflowers. I'll have to look it up when I'm home, use it for the title of an essay about her.

Mom died on Easter, four weeks tomorrow, which (I keep remembering) will be Mother's Day. Every thought and sensation about her death is different than I'd imagined. Till this day on the stream, I've been mostly numb, the action period before mourning sets in. She was seventy-nine, had been sick—we all saw it coming—but none of that matters. I cried over her body, and I cried driving around my old hometown the next day, and I cried at her memorial service when we sang "For the Beauty of the Earth." I mean, there in the front row I couldn't sing, couldn't get breath, held my father's dry hand as if he were the one who needed comforting. Shortly thereafter, I had to stand up and give a eulogy, remember her to the large crowd that had turned out, stood in the pulpit of the church I had grown up in (and then at age thirteen, refused to join on some sort of principle around hypocrisy, also the fact that there was no God—at least not one who goes to church). I should have written the eulogy out beforehand, but just spoke, having forgotten or not anticipated that I'd be rather too upset for a convincing performance extempore. And that was the thing, it was not supposed to be a show. It was supposed to be… something else. In the end it was a *bleat*, but from the heart. Well, that's another fiction. The bleating came from my larynx, air and sound waves shaped by my tongue and lips. A week before that, on Easter Sunday, I'd driven down to Connecticut, to the same house I grew up in, barreled down there on the familiar highways, the ride passing like nothing, six hours non-stop, frequent phone calls to my older brother, Randy, who kept saying, "I think you might want to hurry."

And then that she'd died.

I was a couple of hours too late. And of all the sad things that makes me saddest. I said, "Randy, please don't let them take her away till I get there."

He said he wouldn't, and was as good as his word.

I sat alone with her body an hour or so till the funeral home came to take her. She'd been in home hospice, my loyal and valiant dad caring for her, lying in their familiar boudoir in a rented hospital bed. Sudden turn for the worse, all that, starting on Good Friday. She was religious, and that would have meant something to her. I held her lifeless hand (lifeless, but her own), kept feeling a pulse, but it was my pulse I felt, the one she'd given me. I took the Leatherman off my belt and opened one of its blades, cut a little lock of her white, fine hair as carefully as I could, Victorian keepsake. I gazed at her and thought she'd awaken any minute, say some irritable thing: *"Everyone at me always with knives!"*

The funeral-home men needed professional space in which to move her, asked me if I wouldn't prefer to leave. I kissed her forehead in front of them, kissed her several times, almost fell upon her, finally left, stood out on the patio in light rain, dusk, a sudden vision of her in her red, red cloak, her church clothes. My older brother emerged, stood beside me. Suddenly, almost as if I had been looking for it, I saw a wingspan down in the deep, as yet unleafed woods behind my parents' property—there's a bird sanctuary down there, a large swamp—pointed it out, white, white. Randy said, "Seagull." I blurted, "Snowy owl." Impossible, of course, but that's what I wanted it to be in honor of white-maned Mom and her wisdom, also her large collection of owl figurines. The bird flew up into the canopy then above it and toward us and over us, a great egret, as it turned out, trailing its legs, a bird I'd never seen in that town, though it wouldn't be uncommon, I suppose. I decided silently I would go ahead and believe it was Mom's soul, some kind of vehicle, and that she or it had waited for me these three hours after her breathing had stopped, even though I don't believe in such things at all, goodbye.

I'm in the wrong place. This is not where I meant to be for my hour of looking: too familiar. I get off the thinking rock, cross Nina Brook (which some years ago I named after a frank, lovely girl up the street who was killed at seventeen in a car crash), a sprite that must have crested late last night; the Temple is sloshing thirty feet up into its mouth. But up-brook it's crossable on submerged stones, which I splash across ungainly. One hour of looking is the plan. Naturalists do it all the time. You sit and watch and move as little as possible in green pants and brown shirt and let the forest come to life around you. Beyond the brook I cross under a row of balsams, property line, duck under the sweeping branches, get rained on, look for the blue jay nest I found active five years back: it's still there, a loose assembly of twigs built on two small branches right at the tree trunk, abandoned. Next, there's nothing to do but beat my way through slash and the thousand little five-year popple saplings arrived after Nina's mother had their woods cut. After that, where a clearing was formed, it's raspberries: one raises one's arms and marches through the prickers. Finally released, I cross an impromptu brooklet in the hoofprints of moose and more saplings and shortly find the exact spot I didn't know I had in mind, a beaver-gnawed and felled and abandoned elm (we have plenty of elm here, but most don't live more than ten or fifteen years even when beaver leave them alone: Dutch elm disease), basal diameter eleven inches, the trunk still attached to the stump so forming a bench, bark sloughing off rotted. Perfect.

I remember to mark the beginning of my hour, look at my watch: 3:30. And I sit, mourner at the nexus of several inviting habitats—not all of them temporal. There's the stream, its further bank visible to me, and then the large field beyond. This side of the flow, obscuring it somewhat, there's a thicket of alders and red-osier willows and dogwood and beavered trees arrayed in a vernal bog. The white ash beside me is in heavy, brown flower, the silver maples downstream all in new, flaccid leaves, the yellow birches and popples and black cherries in palest green, the interspersed balsam firs decked in new pink pinecones. I sneeze and sneeze again, all the fresh pollen in the air. Several leopard frogs plop back into the water at the first explosion, several green frogs, one notch braver, leap at the second. Behind me there's the cut forest, a decent job directed by a licensed forester, many seed trees left standing. At the property line, which has been made plain by the thinning, the older, post-pasture hardwoods resume. Over a rise the next property line is apparent, a queue of huge white pines. People's lots are six, ten, forty, a hundred acres here: it's no longer entirely farmland, but still far from suburbia. I can hear a family of crows up in those dense pine branches making a racket.

I clap my hands and they stop.

To paraphrase Thoreau: nothing quiets the forest like a man.

Let's call it a Quaker silence. We'll wait and see who speaks into it.

The first voice, after a mere four minutes or so, is that of a purple finch—not merely a feeder bird, it would seem—who flies in, lands at the top of a thirty-foot (young) balsam and lets fly with a fluid, uprising trill, one chorus only, slightly hoarse, a kind of announcement. Unsatisfied, perhaps having noticed me as I trained my binocs on him, he quickly flies off. Diesel motor in the distance, north. A little tumble of chickadees flies and hops and flutters into my purview then out, saying their names. I hear hammering to the east, downstream, human, not woodpecker. I even know whose house, come to think of it, a half a mile or so away as the crow flies (and, by golly, you know crows fly there often to raid the compost pile!). He's a surgeon, handy with tools, and he's always building something of a Saturday. I hear a chainsaw to the south. Miles of woods that direction. Another motor, like a Model T starting, one pop at a time gaining speed to the west: no, not a motor but a male ruffed grouse on a stump or wall nearby, beating his wings against his puffed chest in hormone-fueled display. At my feet, Canada mayflower in bloom, more trout lily, several early starflowers, false hellebore just getting started (big, ribbed leaves in a tower), tall meadow rue (still short), a nice planting of yellow violets. I've had the unconscious impression of ferns all around, lots of ferns, but this is not bracken, it's blue cohosh, dozens and dozens of plants—perhaps the biggest colony I've ever seen. I'll bring my daughter (she called Mom Nanny), bring her here in fall to show her the big blue berries, four or five or six per plant. The soil in this spot must be very rich.

There are, in fact, a few fronds unfurling, down closer to the bog, the fiddleheads of New York ferns and ostrich ferns, the latter the one people here collect and eat. My mother had been on the board of the National Hardy Fern Society, I learned writing her newspaper obituary. She was a gardener as well as a woods person. I didn't even know there was a National Hardy Fern Society. I don't even know what a hardy fern *is*. I will have to learn. She was also for a time the president of the Board of Trustees of the New Canaan Nature Center, down in wealthy Fairfield County, Connecticut, where she died. All those kind, effusive people at her memorial service, many of them strangers to me: "I learned so much from your mother." "Your mother taught me *mushrooms*." And repeated often in various wordings, always with a wry wink to acknowledge the trouble Reba sometimes found herself in, the following great truth: "Your mother spoke her mind." She'd spearheaded the building of a large community herb garden at the Nature Center, and that is where my Dad will spread her ashes. He wants to do this entirely alone. I was briefly unhappy about this, the Oedipal drama playing out even after the death of the main point of the essential Freudian triangle. But my friends at the party last night, the women at least, found this wish of Dad's to be alone with his girl at the last very romantic. My friend and former colleague Patricia O'Donnell, who has three kids of her own, said soulfully, "It must have been just *awful* for your father sometimes, sharing her with five of you kids! Five!"

He and my mother met in junior high school when he moved with his family from Kansas City to Liberty, Missouri (playing hillbilly, he says it Missour-uh). They were friends right away and later steadies and got married in her father's church in Antioch when they were nineteen, celebrated (very privately) their *sixtieth* wedding anniversary in November, 2005, never having so much as kissed or held hands with anyone else ever. Except us kids.

And here's that flower again, the one with the leaves divided and whorled. I move slowly so as not to make a scene, reach in my "lumbar pack" again for my *Newcomb's Wildflower Guide*, find no books at all. I've left them back on the thinking rock. Well, I'll do without. At least the rock is on the way home and I can collect them. I once left my copy of the huge *Mushrooms Demystified* on top of Jackson Mountain up by Weld, an all-morning hike, luckily in the fall when few ventured that high, could only return three days later after rain, found the book right where I'd left it, next to an inflorescence of queer purple toadstools, and not much worse for the wetting. I told that story to my mother and she said, "I couldn't keep a field guide two weeks with all you kids in the house." And then, genuinely suspicious, "Was that *my* mushroom book?"

When we were little and acting up she'd say, "I'm going to snatch you bald!" but she never did any such thing. If you were being dramatic about some hurt, she'd say, "I feel for you…but *I can't quite reach you.*" If you complained that a sibling had hit you or cheated you, she'd say, "The big fish eat the little fish and the little fish eat the littler fish." Tough love better than none at all!

No mushrooms up yet. Various dry shelf mushrooms (*elfenbonken* in Finnish, my mother read someplace and reported to me, which means "elf-shelfs"), conks and polypores, all the true mushrooms waiting for the warm-up after this long, hard rain. I love the king bolete in butter, oyster mushrooms with garlic, young puffballs in soup. Down in the bog there's a piece of dimensional lumber, a former 2x10, and it's been floating there so long it has its own colony of mosses and those damn flowers I can't name growing on one end, the whole terrarium in motion across a small pool, swinging back and forth with the slight current, back and forth gently.

"Naming is knowing," as Reba Elaine Pearl Burkhardt Roorbach would say.

Once as a teen I shot back, "Naming is not-knowing." I'd been reading the Buddhists, after encountering *Siddhartha*. And she thought about that, puffed her cigarette (a Kent III 100) and said, "Then not-knowing is a way of knowing." We'd have these long philosophical discussions at the kitchen table at night, my father long in bed. The kitchen table was Mom's headquarters. She had an office, too, once the kids were gone, one of the smaller bedrooms, but the kitchen table was her domain, stacks of gardening books and all kinds of magazines and the *New York Times* Sunday crossword in ink, twenty minutes. And cigarettes, always cigarettes, ashtrays overflowing.

When Randy was a teen he bought a box of cigarette charges someplace, these tiny little white pills. You'd empty a pack of Mom's cigs, squeeze and twist a little tobacco out of just one, insert a charge, repack the tobacco, replace the loaded cig in the pack, put the pack back in the cig drawer with all the other dozens of packs. The explosion could come at any time in the following days or weeks: *BANG!* And then a shout: "Goddamn you kids!" The first twenty times were comical, and, after the initial shock Mom (who never otherwise swore) would laugh as we all five of us came running to see, laugh sitting there with her cigarette shredded right down to the filter, flecks of tobacco all over whatever book she was reading and in her hair. The next hundred times were sadistic, and she didn't laugh, and we ran the other way, but I think what we were trying to do was give Mom a message. The word was out on cigarettes. She never did quit smoking however, not till years after we'd all quit, not till the day she had her heart attack. Her last cigarette, in fact, was in the car outside the emergency room, Norwalk Hospital. Her last years were hooked to increasingly bigger tanks, puffing away at pure oxygen.

I've been sitting twenty minutes or so, long enough that even the shyest birds are coming back into the quiet I caused. Somewhere not far a robin is singing shortened phrases appropriate to the time of day. A common yellow-throat jumps up from his thicket and hops branch to branch, making a sound like metal: *clink, clink*. A chestnut-sided warbler is above in his sector (always near water), working the twigs and leaves for tiny caterpillars. A gang of yellow-rumped warblers passes through quickly, silently, landing on this branch then that, gleaning, hopping, flying. I hear a song like a wheel creaking and know it's a black-and-white warbler, there, *there*, scrabbling and picking at bark on an old black cherry tree dying between me and the stream. A redstart suddenly speaks, and repeats, pompous insistence: *my bog, mine*. White-breasted nuthatch, downy woodpecker, oven-bird, gray-cheeked thrush.

I start looking harder for movement at the various layers of forest but keep getting fooled, three ways. 1. Black flies near my face (the first of the season, not too noisome as yet), which little shadows I mistake for dark birds far away. 2. Close bunches of incipient leaves hanging from a beech, mistaken for large unknown mammals moving in the field across the stream, hundreds of yards away. 3. Floaters in my eyes, little shapes at the edges of my vision, thought by some ophthalmologists to be remnants of amniotic mucosa, darting away like warblers when I go to look.

What a good spot. I've seen weasels back in here, a fisher cat once, several mink in winter, beaver on the stream, muskrat, moose, deer, fox, once even a black bear. I hear there are bobcats, but I haven't yet seen one. And insects, insects in incredible numbers and variety for such a short season, in and out of the water, my favorite perhaps the stingless American pelecinid wasp, the female with her abdomen elongated so much that it's like a coarse needle, used for probing after host larvae in which to lay her eggs.

I turn subtly as I can on my butt on the log—turn as slowly as a minute hand—lift my legs over and around, gaze at the hardwoods. A fragrance of garlic arises, and I realize I'm crushing the scimitar leaves of a patch of ramps; or wild leeks, very delicate flavor in soups, rare.

Mom always had something simmering in a little pot on the stove, not to eat, but for fragrance: cinnamon sticks, allspice berries, cloves. At our "bereavement session" at the New Canaan Congregational Church, the kindly associate minister asked for memories of Reba. Randy right away said, "Cooking. I remember cooking with Mom. And nature. She always had a pinecone or a leaf with a bug on it or some rock to show you."

"Small things," my older-younger sister, Carol, said. "Connections between things. All the little things you wouldn't notice."

"Season tickets to the Philharmonic," my younger-younger sister, Janet, sobbed.

"Not when I was a kid!" Randy said. He and I have often observed that there were two families, really, the older one and the younger one, the former less well-to-do than the latter. Randy and I like feeling deprived—the kids who had to beg for the car in high school and drive my father to the station at 5:45 versus the kids who had their own stinking cars. And for me, at least, there are two Moms, the young one with black hair always wrapped up in a towel after a steamy shower, full of hugs and books to read aloud, and the older one with the white, white hair, more acerbic, even mean. Both puffed cigarettes constantly. For my daughter, sadly, only five years old, there's just the deflated old lady in the hospital bed, various locations, weak and often tired, connected to tubes, but always ready to joke and laugh with the little girl, even wheezing. (In her late dementia, Mom thought it was my daughter who had the heart problems, the emphysema, a strange kind of projection, always sure I was protecting her from the truth when I said the girl was fine: "You're being so stoic about it!")

"She volunteered a *lot*," Doug said.

"She *worked*," Janet said. "That was her *work*." And we all nodded at that. Mom was self-tutored, came up in an age when polite women weren't supposed to have advanced degrees or jobs, came of middle age at a time when young women were throwing all that over, a revolution she watched with obvious envy but couldn't quite embrace.

"There's this other thing," Randy said, abstracted, trying to come up with the right word.

My father shifted uncomfortably: he didn't want any secrets spilled in the heart of that old church.

I thought of Mom's sometime sadness, her bouts of depression, her poorly hidden delusions (microphones in lamps, people out to rob her, vast conspiracies peopled by friends and strangers alike), her angry weariness.

"Well, thank you for your time, Patricia," Pop said to the minister, trying to take control.

"Plenty of time," Patricia said, refusing to relinquish it.

Randy continued: "This kind of surprising...*exuberance*."

"Like suddenly she'd just *dance*!" Janet said.

"Me and Bobby McGee!" Carol and I belted out in unison. The hoarse Janis Joplin hit, written by Kris Kristofferson, had been Mom's anomalous theme song back when it was fresh. She'd play it full blast to wake us for school, seven in the morning, turn up the volume when it came on the car radio, windshield wipers slapping time.

On the log, I begin to weep. Not the wracking sobs of the night before, but more gentle, in keeping with the setting. My mother's brother Bobby, the kid closest to her—they were from a family of eight children—died of polio at age five. "*Me and Bobby, me and Bobby McGeeee, yeah!*"

I have to write some of this down. I've left my little reporter's notebook on the rock back there, too, but have a pen in my pocket and the United States Geological Survey topographical map for our area with its big white margins. And I start to write, just write what I'm thinking about, quickly filling the border and moving down into the green areas of the well-worn map, my awful handwriting across Varnum Pond and Derby Mountain, tears falling as on a love letter.

I'm not able to believe in a concrete afterlife. No Pearly Gates or last judgment or gray-bearded God or anything like that. No old friends or beloved family waiting with wings on. I'm not like my late Grandmother Roorbach, widowed at fifty, who, when I as a young boy asked her if she wanted to marry again, said, "*Well*. Several nice gentlemen have asked me, but I always say no. Because, *land sakes alive*, what would I tell Ed when I saw him in Heaven?"

I think my Mom had some belief in all that, too. Her father, her two living brothers, one of her older sisters, were all ministers. In the intensive care unit at Bridgeport Hospital after a very bad week (the week, in fact, that sent her into home hospice) a little more than a year before her final moment (just last month as I sit on the log), I sat up with her all night, thinking it a death vigil. But around four in the morning she regained consciousness, slowly recognized me. She looked stricken, afraid. "Am I dying?" she asked, all urgent.

I didn't want to say yes, in case it wasn't true. Instead, I struggled to sit forward in the comfortable kidney-dialysis lounger a kindly nurse had found me and said, "Do you want to? Are you ready? It would be okay to let go, if you want. Okay to hang on, too, hang on and stay."

And she visibly pulled herself up, visibly girded herself for further battle, said, "Oh, I couldn't die. I would *miss* everybody too much."

The forest around me seems full of vital information. I want to ask questions, *questions*! I take notes on my map, writing across the cartographer's Temple Stream and atop all the surrounding hills and mountains, speaking to the place by writing upon it, the best I can do by way of prayer:
 ...*What I guess I believe is that reincarnation is real, at least on the molecular level. Matter cannot be destroyed, gets reused endlessly. Has Mom's spirit touched the molecules she borrowed somehow?*
No answer.
Does she somehow linger therein all but forever?
No answer.
Is the virtual eternity of matter supposed to be Heaven?
I don't see how. I guess I don't need to see how. In my child-brain there's still a picture of Paradise and it comes unbidden, clouds and gowns and harps and wings, maybe a little boredom. Then again, maybe *this* is Heaven: just a log in the woods with all these temporary molecular assemblages around me, some of them flying, some rooting, some swimming, some abiding as rock, some flowing past on the Temple's flood, all ready to disassemble at a moment's notice, molder down unto earth, explode back into star stuff.

Behind me there's a scuffling, a popping like footsteps. I turn and scan the woods at the height my ears have picked—is someone coming?—but through a kind of miraculous hundred-yard window through everything between us I spy a woodpecker, a female pileated, bright red crest (pileated just means having a cap). She's knocking on an old black cherry trunk so rotten it doesn't resonate. It's still massive, a stub full of woodpecker holes, the bark shearing off in long planches, fungal strands off-white beneath. Our girl's working hard, knocking, resting, picking carpenter ants out of the wreckage, knocking, resting. She stops, seems to brace herself. Waits. The whole forest waits. And suddenly the stub gives way just above her position, gives way and falls. The woodpecker doesn't flinch, not at all, she's seen this before, just cocks her head, examines the break, begins picking off ants.

Tree fall, that's all, but it puts me back among the quick, back in all the birdsong. High in one of the forester's preserved white ashes, a blue-headed vireo (what my mom called a solitary vireo) starts his song, beautiful phrases at slightly better than two-second intervals. And a sudden trill right in front of me, at the very end of a hemlock branch, perfect lighting: pine warbler. I don't even need the books. Scarlet tanager, chickadee male, kingfisher flying past on the stream chattering. Keening of a broad-winged hawk unseen, the chortling of a wild turkey distant, those crows again, high in the white pines. Then there's a strange, loud song from behind. I slowly turn back toward the bog. Two notes, impossibly loud: what weird bird?

No bird.

It's a spring peeper, an exuberant single frog who can't wait for nightfall. Kingbird on the stream. Red-winged blackbirds across, defending territories. Turkey vulture in the sky. Yellow warbler, finally, there he is. That common yellowthroat, singing again, repeating himself: *witchety, witchety, witchety, witch*. But what is that plant, that exquisite five-petal flower, leaves divided, whorled?

Windflower. That's it, the name coming out of nowhere. The plant is a windflower, will only last a while.

Jacob Newberry

Outdoor Sermon on the Concrete Foundation of What Was the First Baptist Church of Gulfport, Mississippi

I walked five hours yesterday and was tired
I grumbled about the heat
        grumbled that I have one pair of shoes now
      grumbled that I'd have to preach on Sunday   in jeans   with no building

        Jesus spoke to me   said, *Do this for thirty years then we can talk*
It was this hot in Judea   in the year thirty-three
Stay outside this long and drag a cross to Golgotha then we can talk

I grumbled about my car being in the ocean
He said
     Give all you have to the poor then we can talk
That's when I thought   yesterday   I could talk back to God
All my things washed away on Tuesday I said
     You have your shoes He told me
     You have your lungs

So I kept walking
There was a woman sifting through driftwood and sand
I asked   What are you looking for?
     my daughter's wedding ring   she said   *it must be here*
     it must be here

I looked through the driftwood too
she said it had been her daughter's house
     her daughter called her early Tuesday morning   in the dark
had gone to the second floor when the waters kept rising
then she was in the attic   said to her, *Mama, I'm putting my ring in the safe for you*

said,   *Mama, there's nowhere left to go*
I looked with her two hours for the ring
     she saw mine   she knew I was a preacher somehow

172

Outdoor Sermon on the Concrete...Church of Gulfport, Mississippi

she whispered to me   though no one was there   she whispered
    when God is reaching up from the sea
    when He's spreading out like the horizon
    take your children to the high places   *away from the sand*
    His wrath is only for those who doubt the warnings

Today I have my wedding ring   I have my wife
last night we pushed our shelter beds together
and set our heads beside each other in the dark   like newborns

    this morning we ate with a soldier
who asked me to bless the food
he said,   *Preacher, I have to gather bodies again today*
    would you say a word   *to help me eat?*
I said a silent prayer   before I prayed
    Save us from this salvation   I cried

Have you heard about New Orleans?
the soldier told me they're still drowning over there
    the soldier told me this morning   Did you hear?
    people are saying they're in the Superdome still
They're eating each other   he said   then vomited
he was from Nebraska   the floods come from the river there

The body of God was here Monday night
and now the governor   he flies in helicopters to watch us from above
    what do we look like from a thousand feet?
it's so hot but we're really in His shadow
we have our crosses to drag to Golgotha
we have those bodies to drag to Golgotha

I went to the water   this morning
I prayed for the prayers that went to the bottom of the sea
    sometimes   even with the Lord
we have to help Him hear in the midst of all this dying

Jacob Newberry

I'll walk again today and be tired
I think I'll walk   the rest of my life
    and the thing is
        when I see another child
      playing in insulation where his school used to be
        when I see another man who stops me
    to say *I have only one pair of socks now*
        when I see another woman in her seventies
      sitting on the front porch steps that lead to no house
        this time
I'll talk back to God
say,   *I have my lungs*   *I have my lungs*

Ken Taylor

mowing

it takes me three hours to mow the field

with no tractor and no bush hog. the dog

usually follows, looks for deer shit

to roll in or eat. from understanding

or habit he sits at the edge of things

panting in shade and watching me attempt

to make order out of fescue, clover,

kentucky blue. rodin said never think

of surface except as extremity

of volume. so he knew about mowing

too. endless thoughts rise with narrowing laps

of the grass. i wonder if i should plant

millet and attract birds or add fruit trees?

is it rain or lack of rain that adds

colors to the fall leaves? and whichever

it is, did we have or not have enough?

Ken Taylor

the mower blade hits a rock. i run through

the list of things to do, tasks done, issues

with my ex, daughters' appointments, sexy

grace of my wife doing yoga, movies

we want to watch, hopes for auburn football.

i take stock of my redneck quotient, up

now with the addition of a back porch

beer fridge. and i ponder at the number

of days remaining made up of hours

spent fashioning a lawn from a field. i

yawn and yield to the zen of circling.

start in on sorting flotsam and jetsam,

what i voluntarily cast away

and what has been broken off by my wrecks.

※

Winners, Finalists and Contributors

WINNER OF THE KNIGHTVILLE POETRY CONTEST AND PUSHCART NOMINEE

Winning poem: A Red Chair

William Derge's poems have appeared in *Negative Capability*, *The Bridge*, *Artful Dodge*, *Bellingham Review*, and many other publications. He is a winner of the Rainmaker Award sponsored by *Zone 3*. He has received honorable mentions in contests sponsored by *The Bridge*, *Sow's Ear*, and *New Millennium*, among others. His work has appeared in several anthologies of Washington poets including *Hungry as We Are* and *Winners*. He lives in Montgomery Village, Maryland, and is a teacher of English as a Second Language.

WINNER OF THE MACHIGONNE FICTION CONTEST AND PUSHCART NOMINEE

Winning story: Fish Story

Until recently Payne Ratner worked as a copywriter at WCSH TV in Portland, Maine. His plays have been produced in Boston, New York and other locations. Three years ago he returned to his first love, fiction. He is a 2010 Stonecoast MFA graduate. This is his first published story. He is deeply grateful to Debra Spark, Shanna Miller McNair and the staff of *The New Guard*. He lives in New Gloucester, Maine, with his two sons.

2010 CONTEST JUDGES

Donald Hall has published fifteen books of poetry, most recently *White Apples and the Taste of Stone* and *The Painted Bed*. He has also written many children's books, notably *Ox-Cart Man*, which won the Caldecott Medal. His works of memoir include *String Too Short to Be Saved*, *The Best Day the Worst Day: Life with Jane Kenyon* and *Life Work*, which won the New England Book award for nonfiction. He was poetry editor for *The Paris Review* from 1953 to 1962 and has edited more than two dozen anthologies and textbooks. Hall was US Poet Laureate in 2006. He has received numerous honors, including the Ruth Lilly Poetry Prize for his lifetime achievement in poetry.

Debra Spark is author of the novels *Coconuts for the Saint* (Faber&Faber, Avon) and *The Ghost of Bridgetown* (Graywolf) and editor of the anthology *Twenty Under Thirty: Best Stories by America's New Young Writers* (Scribners). She is the author of *Curious Attractions: Essays on Fiction Writing* (University of Michigan

WINNERS, FINALISTS AND CONTRIBUTORS

Press) and the novel *Good for the Jews*, which won the 2009 Michigan Literary Fiction Award. *The Pretty Girl*, a collection of stories about art and deception, will be published in 2012 by Four Way Books.

FINALISTS NOMINATED FOR THE PUSHCART PRIZE

ALYSSA BARRETT received a BA from Vassar College and is currently pursuing an MFA in Creative Writing at Columbia University, where she also teaches an undergraduate fiction workshop. Her short stories have appeared in *Helicon* and *The Columbia 2010 Thesis Anthology*. She is originally from western New York and will soon cross the country to live in Washington State. She is at work on a collection of stories about human relationships and connections to the natural world. Alyssa Barrett was nominated for her work of fiction, *The Habits of Phonies and Living Things [Exhibits]*.

KEVIN CAROLLO teaches world literature and writing at Minnesota State University Moorhead. He has poems in *Cream City Review*, *Conduit*, *Court Green*, *Ellipsis*, and elsewhere. He writes for *Rain Taxi Review of Books*, rocks with The New Instructions, and lives in Fargo, North Dakota. Kevin Carollo was nominated for his poem, *Collateral*.

KEN TAYLOR lives and writes in North Carolina. His poetry has also appeared in *The Chattahoochee Review*, *The Stony Thursday Book*, *The Fish Anthology*, *elimae* and *MiPOesias*. He was a Fish Poetry Prize runner-up. He is thankful to *The New Guard* for his Pushcart Prize nomination. Ken Taylor was nominated for his poem, *mowing*.

MATT MILLER was born and raised in Lowell, Massachusetts. He has taught writing workshops at many places including Stanford University, Harvard Extension and the NH State Prison for Men. He has published work in *Slate*, *Harvard Review*, *Notre Dame Review*, and *Memorious* among others. His first book, *Cameo Diner: Poems*, was published in 2005. He is a former Wallace Stegner Fellow in Poetry. He teaches English and coaches football at Philips Exeter Academy and co-directs the Writers' Workshop at PEA. He lives in Exeter, New Hampshire, with his wife, Emily Meehan, and their children, Delaney and Joseph. Matt Miller was nominated for his poem, *Asante*.

Winners, Finalists and Contributors

MACHIGONNE FINALISTS

ALLISON ALSUP is a native of the SF Bay area. Pieces from her emerging historical novel have recently won the *New Millennium*'s Short Short Story Award, A Room of Her Own Foundation's Orlando Award, and most recently the *Philadelphia Stories* Marguerite McGlinn Award. Her stories have been selected as finalists in the 2010 *Salamander* Fiction Contest and 2009 and 2010 Long Fiction Contests, for which she will serve as this year's final judge. White Eagle Coffee Store Press will publish her story, *Oven*, in chapbook form this winter. She lives with her husband in New Orleans. Allison would like to thank *The New Guard* for their encouragement.

ERICA PLOUFFE LAZURE is writer and teacher in Exeter, NH. Her work has appeared or is forthcoming in *McSweeney's Quarterly Concern #29*, *Greensboro Review*, *Meridian*, *Consequence*, *North Carolina Literary Review*, *Mississippi Quarterly*, *Keyhole* and elsewhere. She was the 2009–10 George Bennett writer in residence at Phillips Exeter Academy in New Hampshire and is a graduate of the Bennington Writing Seminars MFA program. *The Cold Front* was selected by C. Michael Curtis in 2008 for the Brenda L. Smart short fiction contest at N.C. State University (the prize did not include publication).

JEFFERSON NAVICKY'S work has appeared in *Quickfiction*, *Smokelong Quarterly*, *Tarpaulin Sky* and others. Black Lodge Press published his chapbook, *Map of the Second Person*. His play, *Lungfish*, appeared in the 2010 Maine Playwright's Festival. He teaches English at Southern Maine Community College, and lives in Portland. *The Air Around Her Objects* is part of an in-progress collection entitled *The True Outskirts of Home*.

JUDITH PODELL was an IRS lawyer for 30 years, hence an abiding fascination with Kafka. Her earliest publication, a feminist satire of *Deep Throat*, appeared in the *Village Voice* in 1973. More recently, her work has been published in the humor anthologies *More Mirth of a Nation: A collection of the best in Contemporary Humor* and *May Contain Nuts*. She is the author of the short story chapbook *Blues for Beginners: Stories and Obsessions*. She holds a USM-Stonecoast MFA. She has been awarded fellowships and grants from the Virginia Center for the Creative Arts, Ragdale Foundation, the MacDowell Colony and the DC Commission for the Arts and the Humanities. She lives in Washington, DC.

Winners, Finalists and Contributors

HEATHER A. SLOMSKI'S work has appeared in *TriQuarterly*, *American Letters & Commentary*, *Columbia*, *Poet Lore* and other journals. She held the Axton Fellowship in Fiction at the University of Louisville from 2008 to 2010. She currently lives in northern Minnesota with her husband and her dog.

J. PRESTON WITT is a writer and professionally trained actor from Flint, Michigan. He holds a BA from the University of Michigan and was a 2010 fellow in the Program for Humanities Development at The Ohio State University. He currently performs, writes, and resides in Paris, France.

KNIGHTVILLE FINALISTS

EILEEN ANNIE is the author of *Life On A Beanstalk: a small collection of ice box poems* (by Eileen A. Schrottke Loos; Bench Press, 1986). Her poems have been published in *Long Island Quarterly* and *Confrontation*. After relocating from Long Island to the Panhandle of Florida, she assumed the position of library director in Franklin County (Florida). She received the 2004 *New York Times* Librarian of the Year Award for outstanding community service. Currently, she is a part-time project director for at-risk teen programs focusing on life skills, career, academic, and creative development.

MICHAEL BAZZETT'S poems have appeared in *West Branch*, *The Literary Review*, *Best New Poets*, *Green Mountains Review*, the *National Poetry Review*, *DIAGRAM*, and *32 Poems*, among others. He was the winner of the 2008 Bechtel Prize from *Teachers & Writers Collaborative*, and an excerpt from his novel for young readers, *Marley Barbeau*, recently appeared in *Hunger Mountain*. New poems are forthcoming in *Bateau*, *Sentence*, *Beloit Poetry Journal* and *10x3*. He lives in Minneapolis with his wife and two children.

DAVID CREWS' poems have appeared or are forthcoming in *The Greensboro Review*, *Paterson Literary Review*, *Exit 13*, *Edison Literary Review*, the anthology *Voices from Here*, and others. He is a 2009 Green Heron Poetry Project winner, and an Honorable Mention in the 2010 Allen Ginsberg Poetry Awards. He received an MFA in Poetry from Drew University, and both teaches and lives in New Jersey.

Poet and writer JEN KARETNICK is the author of six books, including the chapbook *Bud Break at Mango House*, which won the Portlandia Prize. Her poems have appeared in journals including *Alimentum*, *Carpe Articulum*, *Cimarron Review*,

Winners, Finalists and Contributors

North *American Review*, *River Styx* and others. She works as the dining critic for *MIAMI Magazine*, a columnist for *Biscayne Times* and is the Creative Writing Director for Miami Arts Charter School. She has a forthcoming cookbook, *Tales from Mango House*. She lives in Miami on the remains of a historic mango orchard with her husband, two children, three cats, four dogs and fourteen mango trees.

Lynn McGee's poetry has appeared in the *Kennesaw Review*, *Ontario Review*, *Painted Bride Quarterly*, *Sun Magazine*, and other journals. Her fiction has appeared in the *Northwest Review*, *Berkeley Fiction Review* and elsewhere. Lynn's chapbook, *Bonanza*, won the *Slapering Hol* national manuscript contest. She also won the Judith's Room Emerging Writer's Contest in NYC, a MacDowell fellowship, and earned an MFA in Poetry from Columbia. Lynn lives with her partner and 11-year-old stepson in Long Island, New York.

Harry Newman's poems have appeared in numerous publications, including *Ecotone*, *Rattle*, *Asheville Poetry Review* and *Fugue*. His work has been nominated twice for Pushcart Prizes, short-listed twice for the Bridport Prize in England and was second place winner of the William Stafford Award in 2006. In addition to poetry, his plays and translations have been staged in theaters across the US as well as in the Netherlands and Germany.

Michael Pearce's stories and poems have appeared in *Epoch*, *Shenandoah*, *The Gettysburg Review*, *International Quarterly*, *Nimrod*, *Dogwood*, and elsewhere. He lives with his wife and son in Oakland, California, and plays saxophone in the Bay Area bands Highwater Blues and the Delta Dogs.

Elisa Pulido's poetry has appeared in numerous journals, including *River Styx*, *The Ledge*, *Another Chicago Magazine*, *Margie*, *The North American Review* and *RHINO* in the US, and in *Interchange* and *The New Welsh Review* in the UK. In 2007, she was made an honorary member of Academi Cardiff, the national literary society of Wales. She is currently pursuing a doctoral degree in North American Religions at Claremont Graduate University's School of Religion.

Michael Schmeltzer earned an MFA from the Rainier Writing Workshop at Pacific Lutheran University. He helps edit *A River & Sound Review* and is a three-time Pushcart Prize nominee. His work appears or is forthcoming in *Natural Bridge*, *Water~Stone Review*, *New York Quarterly*, *Crab Creek Review*, and *Fourteen Hills*, among others.

WINNERS, FINALISTS AND CONTRIBUTORS

CARY WATERMAN is the author of four books of poems. Her last book, *When I Looked Back You Were Gone* was nominated for a Minnesota Book Award. Her next book, *The Memory Palace*, will be published by Nodin Press in 2011. Her poems are included in the anthologies *Poets Against the War*, *To Sing Along the Way: Minnesota Women Poets from Pre-territorial Days to the Present* and *Where One Song Ends, Another Begins: 150 Years of Minnesota Poetry*. In 2009, she received *The Common Ground* poetry award. She currently teaches creative writing at Augsburg College in Minneapolis.

KNIGHTVILLE POETRY SEMI-FINALISTS

ELINOR BENEDICT'S newest poetry collection is *Late News from the Wilderness*, published by Main Street Rag. She won the May Swenson Poetry Award with her first collection, *All That Divides Us*, from Utah State University Press. She is a graduate of Duke University, Wright State University (Ohio), and Vermont College of Fine Arts. A native of the Tennessee mountains, she now divides her time between Florida and Michigan. She has three children and seven grandchildren.

GEORGE DREW was born in Mississippi and raised there and in upstate New York where he currently resides. He is the author of *Toads in a Poisoned Tank*, *The Horse's Name was Physics*, *Turning Point*, *American Cool*, and *The Hand that Rounded Peter's Dome*. He has been nominated twice for a Pushcart Prize, and has won several magazine poetry awards. *American Cool* won the 2009 Adirondack Literary Award for best poetry book that year. A fifth collection, *The View from Jackass Hill*, won the 2010 X. J. Kennedy Poetry Prize and is forthcoming in 2011.

HAL LACROIX is author of the book *Journey Out of Darkness: The Real American Heroes in Hitler's POW Camps*. He has written for newspapers, magazines and nonprofits; at any moment he will finish his new book about the future. LaCroix lives in the Boston area with his wife, Elahna.

RACHAEL LYON grew up in Nashville, Tennessee. She holds an MFA in Creative Writing from George Mason University and received a 2009–10 Fulbright grant to translate poems from German to English in Vienna, Austria. Her poems have appeared or are forthcoming in such journals as *The Hopkins Review*, *Blue Earth Review*, *Cider Press Review*, and *The Midwest Quarterly*, among others. At work on her first collection of poems, she teaches at Penn State Altoona.

JODIE MARION is from the Indian River region in Florida but has called the Northwest home for the past decade. There, she teaches at a community college, rears four young children, and is a student of the Attic Atheneum Master Writing Program in Portland, Oregon.

JACOB NEWBERRY is a second-year student at Florida State University, pursuing a Ph.D. in Creative Writing, with an emphasis in poetry. His work has been published or is forthcoming in *Rattle*, *Pinyon*, and *Contemporary American Voices*, among others. He is the Poetry Editor at the *Southeast Review*, as well as Associate Editor for the online literary magazine *Juked*.

MARCIA POPP is a retired university professor and the author of several textbooks, biographies, and the poetry collection *comfort in small rooms*. She received the 2008 Robert G. Cohn Prose Poetry Award for the title poem, and a poem from the collection was anthologized by Mark Strand in *Best New Poets 2008*. Another poem from the collection was featured by Garrison Keillor on *The Writer's Almanac* in 2010.

CHRISTINA M. RAU teaches English full time at Nassau Community College and runs Poets In Nassau, a poetry reading circuit on Long Island in New York. Her poetry has most recently appeared in *Potomac Review* and *River Poets Journal*, and she is guest editor of the 2011 forthcoming *Long Island Sounds Anthology*. She is absurdly obsessed with reality television, and she loves moonbeams, puppies, and of course, sarcasm.

THOREAU RAYMOND is a writer and naturalist. Her poetry has appeared in the following publications: *Southern Humanities Review*, *13th Moon: A Feminist Literary Magazine*, *Phoebe*, *The Comstock Review*, *Lucid Stone*, *Poetry Motel*, *The American Journal of Nursing* and *Rough Places Plain: Poems of the Mountains*. She has a poem forthcoming in the June 2011 issue of *Appalachia*.

PENELOPE SCAMBLY SCHOTT'S most recent poetry collection is *Crow Mercies* (2010), winner of the Sarah Lantz Memorial Award from Calyx Press. Her verse biography *A is for Anne: Mistress Hutchinson Disturbs the Commonwealth* was awarded the Oregon Book Award for Poetry in 2008.

BRADFORD WINTERS is a writer and producer in television whose work has ranged from HBO's award-winning series, *Oz*, to the more recent *Kings* on NBC. Based

WINNERS, FINALISTS AND CONTRIBUTORS

in New York City where he's been with The Levinson/Fontana Company for the past twelve years, he is currently developing a feature film called *Americatown*. His poems and essays have appeared or are forthcoming in *Image*, *Spoon River Poetry Review*, and *Tor House*. He is a regular contributor to "Good Letters" on the *Image* website.

JAMES K. ZIMMERMAN is the winner of the 2009 Daniel Varoujan Award and the 2009 & 2010 Hart Crane Memorial Poetry Awards. His work appears or is forthcoming in *Westchester Review*, *Bellingham Review*, *Rosebud*, *ICON*, *Hawai'i Pacific Review* and *Earth's Daughters*, among others. Currently a psychologist in private practice, he was a singer/songwriter in a previous life.

WRITERS TO WRITERS: FAN LETTERS TO THE DEAD

SVEN BIRKERTS is the author of seven books of essays and a memoir. His new book, *The Other Walk*, a collection of memoiristic reflections, will be published in 2011 by Graywolf Press. He edits the journal *AGNI* at Boston University and is Director of the Bennington Writing Seminars.

ADAM BRAVER is the author of four novels, most recently *November 22, 1963*. His books have been selected for the Barnes & Noble Discover program, Border's Original Voices series, and the IndieNext list. He is writer-in-residence and a faculty member at Roger Williams University, as well as writer-in-residence at the NY State Summer Writers Institute.

BOMAN DESAI grew up in Bombay, but has lived his adult life mostly in Chicago. He was set to become a market analyst when a chance encounter with Sir Edmund Hillary, his earliest hero, brought him back to his vocation: writing novels. He took a number of part-time jobs ranging from bartending to teaching in order to find time to write. His first break came when an elegant elderly woman personally submitted his stories to the editor-in-chief of *Debonair* magazine in Bombay. The stories were all published, but the woman vanished, and her identity remains a mystery to this day. He has since published fiction and non in the US, UK, and India, won some awards, taught at some universities, and published some novels. Among other things, he is an amateur musician and Brahms scholar.

Winners, Finalists and Contributors

ANNIE FINCH is the author of many books of poetry, translation, and poetics, including *Calendars*, *Eve*, *Among the Goddesses: An Epic Libretto in Seven Dreams*, and *The Body of Poetry*, as well as a CD version of *Calendars* and creative collaborations merging poetry with music, visual art, and theater. She lives in Portland, Maine, where she is Director of the Stonecoast MFA program at the University of Southern Maine.

JOHN GOLDBACH'S writings have appeared in *Hobart*, *Descant*, *Matrix*, the *Globe and Mail*, the *Coming Envelope* and *Green Mountains Review*, and he is the author of *Selected Blackouts*, a collection of short stories. He lives in Montreal, Quebec.

TOM GRIMES is the author of five novels, a play, and *Mentor: A Memoir*, which is about his friendship with Frank Conroy. He edited *The Workshop: Seven Decades* from the Iowa Writers' Workshop, and he directs the MFA Program in Creative Writing at Texas State University.

RICHARD HOFFMAN is author of three poetry collections, *Without Paradise*, *Gold Star Road*, winner of the 2006 Barrow Street Press Poetry Prize and the New England Poetry Club's Sheila Motton Book Award, and the forthcoming *Emblem*, as well as *Half the House: a Memoir*, and *Interference & Other Stories*. He teaches at Emerson College, and currently serves as Chair of PEN New England.

MAXINE KUMIN'S 17th poetry collection, *Where I Live: New and Selected Poems 1990–2010*, was published by Norton. Also in 2010, Northwestern University Press published *The Roots of Things: Essays*, and Candlewick Press brought out a children's book, *What Color Is Caesar?* Her awards include the Pulitzer and Ruth Lilly Poetry Prizes, the Aiken Taylor Award, the Poets' Prize, and the Harvard Arts and Robert Frost Medals. A former US Poet Laureate, she and her husband live on a farm in central New Hampshire with three rescued dogs and two very old horses.

THOMAS LYNCH'S collection of stories, *Apparition & Late Fictions* and fourth collection of poems, *Walking Papers*, were published by W. W. Norton last year (2010). His nonfiction collections include *The Undertaking*, which was a finalist for the National Book Award. He lives in Milford, Michigan, and Moveen, West Clare, Ireland.

WINNERS, FINALISTS AND CONTRIBUTORS

JOSIP NOVAKOVICH moved from Croatia to the US at the age of twenty. He has published a novel, *April Fool's Day*, three story collections (*Infidelities: Stories of War and Lust*, *Yolk*, and *Salvation and Other Disasters*) and two collections of narrative essays. He has received the Whiting Writer's Award, a Guggenheim fellowship, two National Endowment for the Arts fellowships, the Ingram Merrill Award, and an American Book Award, and he has been a writing fellow of the New York Public Library.

Raised in upstate New York and Maine, LEWIS ROBINSON is the author of the novel *Water Dogs* (Random House, 2009) and *Officer Friendly and Other Stories* (HarperCollins, 2003), winner of the PEN Oakland/Josephine Miles Award. His short fiction and essays have appeared in *Sports Illustrated*, *Tin House*, *The Missouri Review*, *The New York Times Book Review* and on NPR's program *Selected Shorts*. He has received a Whiting Writers' Award, the Glenn Schaeffer Prize, and a National Endowment for the Arts Literary Fellowship. He teaches in the Stonecoast MFA program at the University of Southern Maine and is the writer-in-residence at Phillips Academy in Andover, Massachusetts.

AFAA MICHAEL WEAVER is a poet, playwright, and fiction writer. His eleventh collection of poetry is *Like the Wind*, a translation of his work into Arabic by Wissal Al-Allaq for the Kalimah Project in the UAE. Weaver's website is www.afaamweaver.com.

SCOTT WOLVEN is the author of *Controlled Burn* (Scribner). Wolven's stories have appeared seven years in a row in *The Best American Mystery Stories* series (Houghton Mifflin), the most consecutive appearances in the history of the series. The title story from *Controlled Burn* appeared in *The Best American Noir of The Century* (Houghton Mifflin), edited by James Ellroy and Otto Penzler. Wolven's novels *False Hope* and *King Zero* are forthcoming in 2011. He is finishing another collection of short stories. Wolven's work was featured at 2010 Festival America in Vincennes, France, in *Vintage America* (Albin Michel), with the French photographer Patricia de Gorostarzu and a preface by Clint Eastwood's son, Kyle. He has been a visiting writer at Binghamton (SUNY), Indiana University East and The University of Chicago and is on the faculty of the Stonecoast MFA Program, University of Southern Maine. Wolven lives in upstate New York.

WINNERS, FINALISTS AND CONTRIBUTORS

NEW ESSAYS

JAED COFFIN is the author of *A Chant to Soothe Wild Elephants* (Da Capo/Perseus), a memoir which chronicles his experience as a Buddhist monk in his mother's native village in Thailand. Jaed has spoken widely at universities and colleges where his book is taught as a common text in multicultural curriculum initiatives. Jaed's next book, *Roughhouse Friday* (Riverhead/Penguin), is about the year he fought as the middleweight champion of a barroom boxing show in Juneau, Alaska. Recently, Jaed has served as the 2009 William Sloane Fellow at Bread Loaf Writers Conference, the 2009–10 Wilson Fellow in Creative Writing at Deerfield Academy, and the 2008 Resident Fellow at the Island Institute in Sitka, Alaska. Jaed currently lives and writes in Portland, Maine, and teaches at Stonecoast.

BILL ROORBACH lives and writes in western Maine. He's the author of eight books of fiction, nonfiction, and instruction, with a new novel coming from Algonquin in 2011. He's won the Flannery O'Connor Prize, an O. Henry Award, an NEA grant, the Maine Prize in Nonfiction, and a Kaplan Foundation grant. Find him on the web at billanddavescocktailhour.com and billroorbach.com. Bill, like all men (at least according to Ralph Waldo Emerson), is a god in ruins.

Acknowledgments

The New Guard would like to offer extra thanks to those whose help and support brought this review into being. Everyone who has come on board with *TNG* has been extremely dedicated, without exception.

But first, thank you to all who entered our contests. Submissions were impossibly good and came in an amount nobody expected. Your work inspired us and fueled us throughout the making of this first volume.

A special thanks to our judges, Donald Hall and Debra Spark, whose faith, support and generosity was vital to our launch of *TNG*. And thank you to our winners, finalists and semi-finalists. It is our honor to publish your work.

Thank you to our Fan Letter segment contributors. Each have blessed us with exceptional letters: Sven Birkerts, Adam Braver, Boman Desai, John Goldbach, Tom Grimes, Maxine Kumin, Lewis Robinson, Josip Novakovich and Afaa Michael Weaver. Beyond letters, an extra thank you Richard Hoffman for giving us that extra push, Annie Finch for your unswerving support, Thomas Lynch for the life-affirming gift of time in Moveen, and thank you to Scott Wolven, whose idea for fan letters in this issue was nothing short of extraordinary.

Thank you to our essay contributors, Jaed Coffin and Bill Roorbach, who served up fresh new essays for our inaugural issue.

Thank you to our 2010 Editors, who've been with us since the very start: Erin Enberg for your lyrical sensibility, rare understanding of fiction, and for building bridges between *TNG* and several artists; Melissa Falcon Field for your contagious joie de vivre and ability to see clear to the truth; Brandi Neal for your wonderfully offhanded precision and for always making things easy and Jenny Doughty for your painstakingly careful reading, your wit, your passion for poetry and your natural way of always putting the writers first.

Thank you to Consulting Editor Jesse Miller for your no-bunkum take on things, your unstinting support, your expansive ideas, all those midnight brainstorm sessions and your guiding vision throughout.

Thank you to Jenn Harrington for working tirelessly to make *TNG* all it could be. You are a wonder, and a force of nature. Thank you to Jeremiah Hackett for all your cover mocks, and your good humor throughout. Thank you Sherry Whittemore and David Scribner for being there when we needed you—and for

ACKNOWLEDGMENTS

knowing all kinds of amazing things. Jim Provenzano, we are grateful for your fine art and your one-of-a-kind soulfulness. Kendra Denny, we are thrilled to have your painting on our cover.

A big thank you to the extremely generous George Eadon, aka "Big Cat," who believed in *TNG* from the beginning and made significant and meaningful contributions to this review at a most crucial time during its inception.

Thank you to Catherine Valenza of Portland Arts & Cultural Alliance (PACA), who greatly encouraged us by aligning PACA with *TNG* and becoming our fiscal sponsor, and who also went way out of her way to help personally.

Thank you, thank you to Erin Day, David Lydon, Sarah Schneider, Cindy Williams, Fred Bloom, Zeke Callanan, Liza Provenzano, Josh Bodwell, Tammy Ackerman, Malcolm Cochran, Patrick Rioux, Baron Wormser, April Ossman, Diana Choksey, Margaret Callaghan, Sergei Chaparin, Scott Vaughn at Kase, Portland Arts & Cultural Alliance, its board and good people, Diane McNair, Barbara & Bob Lloyd, our live and virtual fans, and the people of Stonecoast MFA. We would also like to thank Tim O'Sullivan and Jean Hartig of *Poets & Writers*, and *AWP* for their support. A last and very special thank you to Wesley McNair, for making this issue possible.